The Best American History Quiz Book

Tom DeMichael
Sandy Edry
Laura Lee

 Publications International, Ltd.

Tom DeMichael is an award-winning writer/producer in the fields of corporate communications, training, and entertainment. He has authored several books and magazine articles on the subject of American film and is a member of the Chicago Historical Society.

Sandy Edry is a freelance journalist whose articles have appeared in various newspapers and magazines, including *Newsweek*, *The New York Times*, the New York *Daily News*, and Canada's *National Post*. He also spent a year writing for the Emmy-award winning television show *Who Wants to Be a Millionaire*.

Laura Lee is the author of seven books, including *The Pocket Encyclopedia of Aggravations*, *Bad Predictions*, and *Arlo, Alice, and Anglicans: The Lives of a New England Church*.

Facts verified by Karen Collias.

Karen Collias has a Ph.D from Columbia University and an M.Ed. from Boston University, and she has taught history at both the high school and college levels. She has also worked as a historian for the U.S. Department of State.

Cover photos: Superstock (top), Ping Amranand/Superstock (bottom)

Copyright © 2002 Publications International, Ltd. All rights reserved. This book may not be reproduced or quoted in whole or in part by any means whatsoever without written permission from:

Louis Weber, CEO
Publications International, Ltd.
7373 North Cicero Avenue
Lincolnwood, Illinois 60712

Permission is never granted for commercial purposes.

Manufactured in USA.

8 7 6 5 4 3 2 1

ISBN: 0-7853-6259-2

Contents

★ ★ ★ ★ ★ ★ ★ ★ ★

How *The Best American History Quiz Book* Works ★ 4

Americana ★ 5

The Nation's Founders and
the Revolutionary War ★ 19

Explorers and Adventurers ★ 37

Presidential Trivia ★ 49

The Great Depression ★ 69

Pop Culture ★ 83

The Civil War Era ★ 95

Science and Technology ★ 107

The West: Frontier Trivia ★ 117

Military ★ 131

Civil Rights ★ 139

Heroes and Villains ★ 149

Business and the Economy ★ 159

World War II ★ 169

Arts and Literature ★ 181

How *The Best American History Quiz Book* Works

★ ★

A LOT OF HISTORY has accumulated in the United States of America since it was founded more than two centuries ago. If you go back several more centuries to the first European settlement of the new world, there's even more. Once you're out of school and no longer taking tests, it's easy for American history, and all its various facts and tidbits, to slip to the back of your mind.

That's where *The Best American History Quiz Book* comes in. Sure, history class could sometimes seem boring, but at its core, history is full of fun and fascinating information. What really happened on Paul Revere's midnight ride? How much did the first drive-in movie cost? What was J. Edgar Hoover's first name? Is it legal to play pinball in New York City? The answers to these and many other questions can be found in these pages.

The Best American History Quiz Book has 15 chapters, each with its own theme. Start with your favorite subject, maybe the area you think you know the best, and then move on to the others. So you won't accidentally see an answer before you're ready to look, the questions are on one page and their answers are on the next. You'll actually have to turn the page to get an answer.

Quiz your family and friends. Make a challenge out of it, and see who can answer the most questions in a chapter. Answering the questions in *The Best American History Quiz Book* is an enjoyable way to explore American history.

Americana

★ ★ ★ ★ ★ ★ ★ ★ ★ ★ ★

Jazz. Baseball. National landmarks and symbols. They're icons of American life, American ideals, and American culture. They're part of the fabric that makes up this great land. It's called "Americana," and these questions and answers give you a closer look at all things "American."

1. Uncle Sam, dressed in his red, white, and blue top hat and tails, has become the personification of America. True or False: Uncle Sam was based on a real person.

2. Education has always been an important part of American life. What was the first chartered college in the New World?

A. William & Mary
B. Columbia
C. Yale
D. Harvard

3. According to historians and experts, baseball, America's pastime, was invented by whom?

A. Alexander Cartwright
B. Abner Doubleday
C. Albert G. Spalding
D. Cap Anson

Answers

★ ★ ★ ★ ★ ★

1. Answer: True. The real Samuel Wilson was born in Massachusetts in 1766, and he banged a drum during the Revolutionary War. By the War of 1812, Wilson had a meatpacking plant that supplied rations to U.S. soldiers. He stamped his crates with a large *U.S.* on the side, for *United States*. A worker joked that since the crates came from Sam Wilson, *U.S.* really stood for *Uncle Sam*. The joke caught on, and soon everyone refered to *Uncle Sam's* crates. Cartoonists drew Sam as clean-shaven until the 20th century, when he was portrayed as tall and bearded.

2. Answer: D. Harvard. Started in 1636 as an all-male school to educate Puritan ministers, this college had only nine students and one teacher. Today it has grown in enrollment to 18,000 undergraduate and graduate-degree candidates and has become perhaps the best-known educational institution in the world. It was also the alma mater for seven U.S. presidents (both Adamses, both Roosevelts, Hayes, Kennedy, and George W. Bush).

3. Answer: A. Alexander Cartwright. For years, most people believed that Abner Doubleday invented the game in Cooperstown, New York. In actuality, it evolved from English games such as rounders and cricket and came to be called "town ball" in the United States. Young Alexander Cartwright had played that game, and in 1845, he and his team, the Knickerbocker Base Ball Club, wrote down specific new rules, such as three strikes for an out and three outs for an inning. Cartwright was inducted to the National Baseball Hall of Fame in 1938. Doubleday has never been inducted.

QUESTIONS

★ ★ ★ ★ ★ ★ ★

4. Which one of the following people did *not* star on old-time radio?

A. Benjamin Kubelsky
B. Bernie Schwartz
C. Nathan Birnbaum
D. Leslie Towne Hope

5. The colors red, white, and blue are synonymous with the United States of America. While these colors did not have any symbolism when they were chosen for the first U.S. flag, their meaning was explained in relation to the Great Seal of the United States, adopted in 1782. Charles Thompson, Secretary of the Continental Congress, wrote, "White signifies purity and innocence, Red, hardiness and valor." What does blue signify?

A. Truth and honor
B. The freedom of American skies
C. Vigilance, perseverance, and justice
D. Faith, hope, and charity

6. Louis Armstrong certainly was one of the great American jazz musicians. He often went by the nickname of "Satchmo." Where did he get that name?

A. He loved to eat satchmo, an old New Orleans dish of crawfish and beans.
B. "Satchmo" was shortened from "such motion," because he could never sit still.
C. His nickname had been "Satchelmouth," but a reporter in England mispronounced it as "Satchmo."
D. "Satchmo" was a word he said as an infant.

Answers

★ ★ ★ ★ ★ ★

4. Answer: B. Bernie Schwartz. Benjamin Kubelsky was better known as Jack Benny, whose penny-pinching ways amused radio listeners in the '30s and '40s. Nathan Birnbaum was the real name of George Burns, who teamed with his wife, Gracie Allen, to tickle the funny bones of America. Leslie Towne Hope is also referred to as "The Great Ski Nose," alias Bob Hope. Hope not only entertained radio audiences, but was a big star in movies and on television, as well. Schwartz was also a star, but not in radio. Adopting the stage name Tony Curtis, he came along after radio's Golden Age.

5. Answer: C. Vigilance, perseverance, and justice. Although the colors didn't initially have a symbolic meaning, other elements of the flag always did. The 13 red and white stripes represent the original colonies, while the 50 white stars on a blue field each represent a state in the Union.

6. Answer: C. His nickname had been "Satchelmouth," but a reporter in England mispronounced it as "Satchmo." When he was a child, Louis Armstrong's friends called him "Satchelmouth" because they thought his mouth was as large as a satchel. He was also sometimes called "Gatemouth." During an early tour of England, a music journalist shortened it to "Satchmo." Armstrong loved the new name and quickly adopted it.

Questions

★ ★ ★ ★ ★ ★ ★ ★

7. The birth of American suburbia can be traced to 1949, when a 1,500-acre potato field on New York's Long Island was purchased. Thousands of homes erupted like, well—like potatoes in a field. What was the name of this historic development?

A. Yorkington
B. Levittown
C. Terrytown
D. Spudtown

8. The Miss America Pageant began in 1921 as a way to encourage tourists to stay in Atlantic City for another weekend after Labor Day. Through the years, what state has given us the most Miss Americas?

A. Ohio
B. Pennsylvania
C. Florida
D. California

9. True or False: The Pledge of Allegiance was written as part of the oath taken by the Union soldiers during the Civil War.

Answers

★ ★ ★ ★ ★ ★

7. Answer: B. Levittown. William J. Levitt imagined block after block of quiet homes, running along quiet side streets. Apparently so did several thousand buyers, who waited anxiously outside his sales office. For just under $10,000, post-World-War-II Americans could get their own little four-room place—landscaped and filled with appliances. Levitt repeated his suburban success on eight square miles in Pennsylvania, building a densely populated town of 70,000. But by then, builders and developers across the country were copying his idea.

8. Answer: D. California. Seventy-four Miss Americas have worn the crown since the pageant began, and the "Golden State" has been home to six of them. Ohio and Pennsylvania are tied for second with five apiece (although one Ohio winner held the role for two years running). Four states have each had four winners, and Florida, the "Sunshine State," has had only one.

9. Answer: False. The Pledge of Allegiance was written in 1892, intended as a one-time recital for America's schoolchildren to celebrate Columbus Day. The editor of *The Youth's Companion,* Francis Bellamy, was surprised when his verse first became an annual Columbus Day tradition and eventually turned into a daily recitation for schoolchildren across the country. The words "under God" were added in 1954.

QUESTIONS

★ ★ ★ ★ ★ ★ ★

10. From 1926 to 1985, it officially ran from Chicago, Illinois, to Santa Monica, California. What was it?

A. U.S. Route 1
B. U.S. Highway 99
C. U.S. Route 66
D. The Empire Builder

11. Some things are so comfortable and familiar that they seem to have always been a part of American life. But everything has to start sometime and somewhere. Which came first: the American supermarket or the foldable brown paper bag?

12. It might be said that baseball would be nothing without its statistics. Here's one from the early days of the game: Which American League baseball player (with the initials B.R.) led the league in home runs in 1915?

A. Babe Ruth
B. Braggo Roth
C. Billy Russell
D. Bud Rasche

Answers

★ ★ ★ ★ ★ ★

10. **Answer: C. U.S. Route 66.** Emerging from the national need for improved roadways, Route 66 became the first highway to stretch from the Midwest, through the Great Plains and the Southwestern desert, to end at the lip of the Pacific coastline. The 2,248-mile-long roadway became a romantic icon for open-road auto travel in the '50s and '60s. By the time the U.S. Interstate System replaced Route 66 with super-highways in the '80s, millions of riders had gotten their "kicks on Route 66."

11. **Answer: The foldable brown paper bag.** In the early 1880s, paper bags were v-shaped. Charles Stilwell was disappointed that these bags couldn't stand on their own and, being made by hand, sometimes fell apart. Being a "big idea" sort of fellow, he designed a machine in 1883 that would automatically fold and glue a flat-bottomed pleated bag. By contrast, the first generally recognized supermarket in America was King Kullen Grocery, which opened in Queens, New York, in 1930 (properly stocked with plenty of Stilwell's bags, no doubt).

12. **Answer: B. Braggo Roth.** Although Babe Ruth, "The Bambino," had just started his career as a pitcher with the Boston Red Sox, he cracked four homers in 1915. (This was known as the "dead ball era," a time when baseballs were made differently and didn't travel very far when hit, so nobody was hitting very many home runs.) Roth, an outfielder for the Chicago White Sox and the Cleveland Indians, cleared the fences only seven times to lead all American Leaguers in 1915.

QUESTIONS

★ ★ ★ ★ ★ ★ ★

13. Before you go out in the morning, you want to know whether it's hot or cold, sunny or raining, so you'll know what to wear. Most of our weather information comes from the National Weather Service. When was it established?

A. 1856
B. 1870
C. 1900
D. 1923

14. Which of these American historical periods came first?

A. Jazz Age
B. New Deal Era
C. Progressive Era
D. Gilded Age

15. In 1867, a man named William Seward bought something that many people believed was a waste of money. What was "Seward's Folly"?

A. The first steam-powered auto
B. The Brooklyn Bridge
C. The Alaskan Territory
D. The Hawaiian Islands

Answers

★ ★ ★ ★ ★ ★

13. **Answer: B. 1870.** Initially called the National Weather Bureau, it was originally part of the U.S. Army Signal Corps. The bureau's main purpose, as it remains to this day, was to report, predict, and study the phenomena of weather in America. The bureau was moved to the Department of Agriculture in 1891, since the effects of weather had a great impact on America's farmers. In 1940, however, as America moved toward industrialization, it was taken over by the Department of Commerce. It was renamed the National Weather Service in 1970 and placed under the National Oceanic and Atmospheric Administration.

14. **Answer: D. Gilded Age.** The Gilded Age is often remembered as a time of corrupt politics and corporate domination, running roughly from 1878 to 1901, from after the end of Reconstruction until the start of Theodore Roosevelt's presidency. The age took its name from the title of a book by Charles Dudley Warner and Mark Twain.

15. **Answer: C. The Alaskan Territory.** As secretary of state under President Andrew Johnson, William Seward paid Russia $7,200,000 for what many said was "a large lump of ice." But the land was rich with furs, fish, and Klondike gold. At only two cents an acre, some folks just know a bargain when they see one.

QUESTIONS

★ ★ ★ ★ ★ ★ ★

16. Why were baseball's Brooklyn Dodgers (later the Los Angeles Dodgers) called "the Dodgers"?

A. Brooklyn fans had to dodge trolleys to get to the ballpark.
B. The infield was so inept, they had to dodge flying baseballs.
C. Their ace pitcher was Roger "Dodger" McNulty.
D. "Yankees" was already taken.

17. The year is 1954, and you're sitting in front of your first TV set, behind your first TV trays. The first TV dinner has just been introduced to America. What are you having?

A. Fried chicken
B. Salisbury steak
C. Sliced turkey
D. Chateaubriand

18. Mount Rushmore may be the ultimate example of people putting their print onto nature. It's also one of the great monuments to American patriotism. But it might not have been. What three profiles were originally intended for Mount Rushmore?

A. Presidents Washington, Lincoln, and Grant
B. Presidents Lincoln, Garfield, and McKinley
C. Western heroes Kit Carson, Jim Bridger, and John Colter
D. Fabled icons Paul Bunyon, Johnny Appleseed, and John Henry

ANSWERS

★ ★ ★ ★ ★ ★

16. **Answer: A. Brooklyn fans had to dodge trolleys to get to the ballpark.** Washington Park, located in the Red Hook portion of the borough of Brooklyn, served as the home for the Dodgers. Getting to the stadium involved "dodging" the trolley cars of the Brooklyn Rapid Transit Company. In 1912, the Dodgers moved to Ebbets Field in the Brooklyn neighborhood of Flatbush, but by then the name had stuck.

17. **Answer: C. Sliced turkey.** You've also got corn bread dressing and whipped sweet potatoes. Frozen food had been around for about 30 years, but this was the first time an entire meal had been frozen together. Frozen dinners have gone on to change America's eating habits. By the way, the divided aluminum trays were discontinued in 1984—too much sparking in the microwave.

18. **Answer: C. Western heroes Kit Carson, Jim Bridger, and John Colter.** Carson, famed hunter, trapper, and scout; Bridger, pioneering trader and explorer; and Colter, first pioneer to explore the Wyoming territory, were originally proposed for immortalization by a South Dakota historian who thought they would spur tourism. Fortunately, sculptor Gutzon Borglum convinced everyone that "prominent figures," such as presidents, were better suited for 60-foot-high faces. The sculpture was finished by Borglum's son in 1941.

QUESTIONS

★ ★ ★ ★ ★ ★ ★

19. Which of these names was *not* considered for the Christmas holiday's favorite member of Santa's team?

A. Rudolph, the Red-Nosed Reindeer
B. Rollo, the Red-Nosed Reindeer
C. Reginald, the Red-Nosed Reindeer
D. Robespierre, the Red-Nosed Reindeer

20. The Statue of Liberty stands on Liberty Island in New York Harbor. Has it always been called "Liberty Island"? If not, what was its original name?

A. Yes, it's always been called "Liberty Island" and nothing else.
B. No, it was originally called "Bedloe's Island."
C. No, it was originally called "Ellis Island."
D. No, it was originally called "Harbor Island."

21. What state provides the geographic center of the continental United States?

A. Kansas
B. Oklahoma
C. South Dakota
D. Iowa

ANSWERS
★ ★ ★ ★ ★ ★ ★

19. **Answer: D. Robespierre, the Red-Nosed Reindeer.** The other three names sprang from the fertile mind of copywriter Robert May, who was working for Chicago's Montgomery Ward in 1939, developing an illustrated kids' poem for the upcoming holiday season. That Christmas, nearly 2.5 million "Rudolph" books were handed out nationwide. A few years later, songwriter Johnny Marks put the poem to music. In 1949, Hollywood cowboy Gene Autry's version of the song shot to the top of the music charts.

20. **Answer: B. No, it was originally called "Bedloe's Island."** Home to Fort Wood, Bedloe's Island was named for 18th-century New York resident Isaac Bedloe and was selected as the base for the Statue of Liberty when it was assembled in 1886. President Calvin Coolidge proclaimed the island and statue a national monument in 1924. Bedloe's Island was renamed Liberty Island in 1956 under President Dwight Eisenhower.

21. **Answer: A. Kansas.** Specifically, the exact center is near the town of Lebanon, Kansas, which is in the far northern portion of the state, just off the Nebraska border. If you want to include Alaska and Hawaii, then the geographic center moves to a point near Castle Rock, South Dakota, in the west-central portion of the state.

THE NATION'S FOUNDERS AND THE REVOLUTIONARY WAR

The battle for freedom and independence from British rule left America with timeless warriors like Washington, Jefferson, Hamilton, Henry, and Hale. But a lot of other people contributed to this cause as well. How much do you know about what is literally the defining moment of American history?

1. In 1770, who led the colonial protest that resulted in the Boston Massacre?

A. Samuel Adams
B. Crispus Attucks
C. Patrick Henry
D. John Preston

2. Most historians mark April 19, 1775, as the start of the American Revolution, when the "shot heard 'round the world" was fired. Where was that shot fired?

A. Philadelphia, Pennsylvania
B. Trenton, New Jersey
C. Lexington, Massachusetts
D. Boston, Massachusetts

3. About how many people lived in the 13 original colonies at the start of the American Revolution?

A. 500,000
B. 1,000,000
C. 2,500,000
D. 5,000,000

Answers

★ ★ ★ ★ ★ ★

1. **Answer: B. Crispus Attucks.** The son of a Native American mother and an African father, Attucks may have been a runaway slave. His bold 1770 protest against the continuing influx of British troops to the Boston area broke down into a rock-throwing riot against armed soldiers. Some of the British soldiers retaliated with gunfire, which killed Attucks and four other colonists. The soldiers were tried for murder, but either were acquitted or received light sentences.

2. **Answer: C. Lexington, Massachusetts.** British troops, 700 strong, were advancing on Concord to destroy arms and munitions that belonged to the patriots. At Lexington, they found 77 members of the local militia known as "Minutemen." Someone—to this day no one knows who—fired an unordered shot. The gunfire that followed resulted in eight Americans killed and eight wounded. The British pushed on to Concord, but resistance there forced them to return under fire to Boston, their mission a failure. The resulting colonial siege of Boston from the Royal Crown took nearly a year.

3. **Answer: C. 2,500,000.** The population of the colonies, only about 250,000 in 1700, had exploded in the years before the Revolution. But not all of these colonists had come from England. The colonies of New England were predominantly of English descent, but inhabitants of the mid-Atlantic and Southern colonies were made up primarily of German, Scottish, and Irish immigrants.

QUESTIONS

★ ★ ★ ★ ★ ★ ★

4. The war's first major battle, Bunker Hill, came in June 1775. It was here that American Colonel William Prescott gave his famous order: "Don't one of you fire until you see the whites of their eyes." He reasoned that holding fire until the enemy was close would save valuable ammunition for the rebels. The 1,200 colonial soldiers let the 2,200 Redcoats come close before firing, with devastating results. Where did most of this battle take place?

A. Bunker Hill
B. Breed's Hill
C. Boston Hill
D. Blueberry Hill

5. Which British monarch lost the colonies during the American Revolution?

A. William IV
B. Charles II
C. Victoria
D. George III

6. Benjamin Franklin, a statesman, inventor, and author of *Poor Richard's Almanac,* is well remembered for his pithy observations. Which of these quotations is *not* attributed to Franklin?

A. Never leave that till to-morrow which you can do to-day.
B. These are the times that try men's souls.
C. Remember that time is money.
D. There never was a good war or a bad peace.

Answers

★ ★ ★ ★ ★ ★

4. Answer: B. Breed's Hill. The battle was for control of two hills overlooking Boston Harbor: Bunker Hill and Breed's Hill. The Americans had built a defensive enclosure on top of Breed's Hill, and it took the British three tries before they captured it. That capture took a high price—of 2,200 British soldiers, 1,096, almost half, were killed or wounded.

5. Answer: D. George III. 'Twas Mad King George who first lost the colonies and later his mind. The British policies of taxation and coercion sparked the conflict, and George's obstinate refusal to accept American independence prolonged the war. It's been suggested that George suffered from the hereditary disease porphyria and that the strain of the war helped exacerbate his illness. He went permanently insane in 1810 and died ten years later.

6. Answer: B. These are the times that try men's souls. This tidbit belongs to fellow founder and writer Thomas Paine. It is the opening line to a series of pamphlets first published in December 1776 called *The American Crisis*. The English-born Paine went on to write several other influential books, including *The Rights of Man*, a defense of the French Revolution, and *The Age of Reason*, which he wrote while imprisoned in a French jail.

QUESTIONS

★ ★ ★ ★ ★ ★ ★

7. An international group of soldiers and other military men came from a variety of countries to help the United States win its independence. General Lafayette of France is the most famous. True or False: The Revolutionary Army included officers from Germany and Poland.

8. The band of soldiers calling themselves the Green Mountain Boys took their name from the Green Mountains of which present-day state?

A. New York
B. New Hampshire
C. Vermont
D. West Virginia

9. True or False: The actual document known as the Declaration of Independence still exists today.

Answers

★ ★ ★ ★ ★ ★ ★

7. Answer: True. Both countries made a contribution to the effort. Poland provided the expertise of Thaddeus Kosciusko and Count Casimir Pulaski. Kosciusko, a military engineer, directed construction of forts at West Point and New York, while Pulaski led many raids with American and French troops. German Baron Friedrick von Steuben was named inspector general of the army. A skilled trainer of troops, he became a United States citizen in 1783 and received a governmental pension.

8. Answer C. Vermont. Organized to prevent a New York claim on the region, armed groups led by land speculators like Ethan Allen and his brothers used intimidation and violence to keep the area out of New York's control. The Green Mountain Boys achieved the colonies' first war victory, capturing Fort Ticonderoga on May 10, 1775. (Truth be told, that "victory" mostly consisted of walking through the gates and taking over while the British slept.) In 1777, Vermont proclaimed itself an independent state, but the Continental Congress didn't recognize it as such until 1791 when it became the 14th state of the Union.

9. Answer: True. Adopted on July 4, 1776, the parchment moved from the State Department to the Library of Congress before becoming the responsibility of the National Archives in 1952. It actually accompanied the Continental Congress wherever it met during the Revolution and in the early years of the republic. Faded somewhat due to poor preservation techniques, today it can usually be found in the National Archives Exhibit Hall, nestled in an airtight container.

QUESTIONS

★ ★ ★ ★ ★ ★ ★ ★

10. The first flag of the American nation, with its 13 red-and-white stripes and 13 stars circling in the blue box in the left-hand corner, has inspired a lot of people over the years. True or False: Betsy Ross designed that first American flag.

11. The colonists were never fond of the taxes imposed by the British government. After a number of tax acts were passed by Parliament, the British tax on tea imported to the colonies was the straw that broke the camel's back. One night in December 1773, a group of Boston patriots boarded three Royal vessels and tossed almost 400 chests of tea into Boston Harbor. What American patriot led the Boston Tea Party?

A. Paul Revere
B. John Adams
C. John Jay
D. Samuel Adams

12. Before the Revolutionary War, the British had been active in exploring North America. During the war itself, how far west could British troops be found?

A. Iowa and Kansas territory
B. Illinois and Kentucky territory
C. Minnesota and Wisconsin territory
D. Nevada and California territory

ANSWERS

★ ★ ★ ★ ★ ★

10. **Answer: False.** Betsy Ross was a seamstress in Philadelphia and is known to have made flags during the Revolution, but the claim that she created the first Stars and Stripes is undocumented and has generally been discredited. No one knows for sure who created the original design, but one likely possibility is writer, musician, and Declaration of Independence signer Francis Hopkinson, who was Chairman of the Navy Board between 1776 and 1778.

11. **Answer: D. Samuel Adams.** Adams, a former tax collector of Boston, was active in many rebellions against British rule. He was outspokenly opposed to the Sugar Act, which taxed and restricted the shipping of sugar and molasses from the West Indies to America. Adams also fought against the Stamp Act, which literally required all printed materials to carry a tax stamp.

12. **Answer: B. Illinois and Kentucky territory.** In 1778, George Rogers Clark, a lieutenant colonel in the Virginia militia (and brother of explorer William Clark), captured British troops in Illinois territory. Famous frontiersman Daniel Boone did the same in Kentucky territory.

Questions

★ ★ ★ ★ ★ ★ ★

13. Schoolchildren through the years have recited the exciting poem by Henry Wadsworth Longfellow, "Paul Revere's Ride." True or False: The real Paul Revere never reached his destination of Concord, Massachusetts, on his midnight ride.

14. Thomas Jefferson was known as the Father of the Declaration of Independence, but which founder was called the "Master Builder of the Constitution"?

A. John Adams
B. John Hancock
C. Alexander Hamilton
D. James Madison

15. Believe it or not, the first submarine ever to be used during a war was on the side of the colonists. What was its name?

A. The *Salamander*
B. The *Iron Shark*
C. The *Turtle*
D. The *Blowfish*

ANSWERS

★ ★ ★ ★ ★ ★ ★

13. Answer: True. Late in the evening of April 18, 1775, Paul Revere and two others left Boston on horseback, rushing to warn residents of Concord that British Redcoats were coming to destroy colonial arms. However, it appears that Longfellow exaggerated Revere's role. British spies detained Revere and another rider, while the third successfully warned Concord of the attack.

14. Answer: D. James Madison. He may have been short of stature, but the 5'4" Madison is a giant in American history. He drafted the "Virginia Plan," which became the basis of the Constitution. Although a poor orator, Madison took the floor more than 150 times at the Continental Congress to push tirelessly for a strong central government. (With Alexander Hamilton and John Jay, he also wrote *The Federalist Papers*, commenting on constitutional issues.) After fighting the likes of Patrick Henry to ensure ratification of the Constitution, Madison was elected to Congress, then appointed secretary of state. He was finally elected president in 1808.

15. Answer: C. The *Turtle*. Inventor David Bushnell built the submersible craft from oak planks and iron bands. With room for only one person, the *Turtle* was hand-powered for propulsion and hand-pumped for respiration. It carried one gunpowder bomb to screw into the hull of an enemy ship. Targeting the British *Eagle* in New York Harbor, the *Turtle* was thwarted by a metal plate in the *Eagle*'s hull, and its bomb couldn't be attached. The mission was abandoned. In a handful of subsequent missions, it was never successful in delivering its bomb.

QUESTIONS

★ ★ ★ ★ ★ ★ ★

16. In late 1777, George Washington needed somewhere to encamp his troops for the winter. Why did he choose to settle in at Valley Forge?

A. It had plenty of food, water, and shelter.
B. It had a clear view of New York City.
C. It was the site of his most recent battle victory.
D. It was easy to defend while protecting the convening Congress.

17. True or False: General Benedict Arnold's acts of treason against the colonies led to his becoming a British hero.

18. Her real name was Mary McCauley Hays. By what name do we know this hero of the American Revolution today?

A. Betsy Ross
B. Martha Washington
C. Molly Pitcher
D. Abigail Adams

Answers

★ ★ ★ ★ ★ ★ ★

16. **Answer: D. It was easy to defend while protecting the convening Congress.** While George Washington certainly had his reasons for choosing this site near Philadelphia, the barren lands provided little shelter from the winter, and many soldiers froze to death or starved from lack of food. By February 1778, however, the army began to regroup.

17. **Answer: False.** General Benedict Arnold, originally skilled as a druggist, earned praise from colonial leaders for his leadership early in the American Revolution. But when he was passed over for promotion and received a court-martial charge for violating military regulations, Arnold went over to the side of the British. He led raids on former allies and friends and sailed for England. But the end of the war meant the end of Arnold's notoriety. The Brits regarded Arnold as just a traitor who couldn't be trusted.

18. **Answer: C. Molly Pitcher.** Molly earned her nickname during the Battle of Monmouth in 1778, when she fetched water for her husband, John Hays, and his gun crew. After her husband suffered a wound, she took over his position for him, helping the gun crew do its job. After the war, she was awarded a yearly pension of $40 by the Pennsylvania Assembly.

Questions

★ ★ ★ ★ ★ ★ ★

19. As an outspoken statesman, Patrick Henry once asked for the choice of liberty or death. Which of these positions did Henry *not* hold?

A. Lawyer
B. Governor of Virginia
C. Storekeeper
D. Secretary of state

20. The Continental Congress that commissioned the Declaration of Independence included representatives from each of the 13 colonies. The Declaration had 56 signers. Which colony sponsored the largest number of them?

A. New York
B. Virginia
C. Pennsylvania
D. Massachusetts

21. What patriot spy is said to have told his British executioners, "I only regret that I have but one life to lose for my country"?

A. Ethan Allen
B. Francis Marion
C. Nathan Hale
D. Mad Anthony Wayne

Answers

19. Answer: D. Secretary of state. Patrick Henry was a self-taught lawyer, and he once ran a store with his older brother. He became the first governor of the commonwealth of Virginia in 1776, an office he held for five terms. But declining health forced Henry to turn down several key governmental positions, including secretary of state under George Washington, Chief Justice of the U.S. Supreme Court, U.S. senator, and U.S. minister to France. Washington convinced Henry to run for the Virginia legislature in 1799, and the great orator won his final campaign. He died before he could take office.

20. Answer: C. Pennsylvania. New York had four signers, while Virginia had eight and Massachusetts, five. But Pennsylvania sent nine signers, including Benjamin Franklin. Among the other signers from the "Keystone State" were James Wilson, an attorney who was eventually named an associate justice of the first U.S. Supreme Court, and Benjamin Rush, one of the most influential physicians in the colonies at the time.

21. Answer: C. Nathan Hale. Hale, a Connecticut teacher before the war broke out, volunteered to find out about British troops on Long Island. Disguised as a Dutch teacher, the 21-year-old army captain made it behind enemy lines but was captured and hanged on September 22, 1776. No one knows for sure if Hale actually spoke these words at the gallows, but it is believed he was familiar with the English writer Joseph Addison and was paraphrasing a line from the play *Cato,* "What pity is it/That we can die but once to serve our country!"

Questions

★ ★ ★ ★ ★ ★ ★ ★

22. Following the triumph of the Revolutionary War, there remained the issue of what the country's new government would govern and how it would do so. The Articles of Confederation, ratified in 1781, had been ineffective, so a new constitution needed to be considered. Where was the Continental Convention of 1787 held?

A. New York
B. Philadelphia
C. Washington, D.C.
D. Boston

23. John Paul Jones was the first American naval hero. Entangled in a fierce battle with the British frigate *Serapis* in 1779, Jones's ship, the *Bonhomme Richard,* had taken severe damage. When the *Serapis*'s captain asked if he was ready to surrender, Jones yelled his immortal response: "I have not yet begun to fight!" Jones won that battle and took over the *Serapis*. In what year was he buried at the U.S. Naval Academy in Annapolis?

A. 1792
B. 1814
C. 1866
D. 1905

24. In addition to his many other accomplishments, Benjamin Franklin was very adept in developing new devices and institutions. Which of these was *not* a Ben Franklin creation?

A. The Franklin stove
B. America's first public library
C. The dumbwaiter
D. The lightning rod

Answers

★ ★ ★ ★ ★ ★ ★

22. **Answer: B. Philadelphia.** Among the 55 delegates present were not-yet-president George Washington, Ben Franklin, Alexander Hamilton, and James Madison. Tossing the Articles of Confederation into the wastebasket, they built a new and stronger form of government. The eventual result was the Constitution (and the accompanying Bill of Rights) and the basis of government structure and operation that still runs today.

23. **Answer: D. 1905.** After the war, John Paul Jones retired to France, where in 1792 he died and was buried in an unmarked grave. His remains were removed from that grave in 1905 and were buried, with honors, at the U.S. Naval Academy.

24. **Answer: C. The dumbwaiter.** That ingenious invention was courtesy of Thomas Jefferson. From an early age, Benjamin Franklin immersed himself in the technical and journalistic facets of printing. He soon became a master printer, as well as writer, publishing *Poor Richard's Almanac* in 1732. Living in Philadelphia, he improved the efficiency of heating with the Franklin stove, started America's first public library, and founded the city's first fire department. His fascination with electricity led to the development of the lightning rod and his famous experiments with lightning and kites in 1752.

QUESTIONS

★ ★ ★ ★ ★ ★ ★

25. Where was the capital of the United States immediately before it moved to Washington, D.C., in 1800?

A. Philadelphia
B. New York
C. Boston
D. Baltimore

26. The surrender of General Charles Cornwallis ended the Revolutionary War. At what Virginia location did the surrender take place?

A. Richmond
B. Williamsburg
C. Appomattox
D. Yorktown

ANSWERS

★ ★ ★ ★ ★ ★

25. **Answer: A. Philadelphia.** A rivalry between Northern and Southern advocates who each pushed to have the capital in one of the states of their region, had kept a permanent location undecided. In 1790 a compromise finally resolved the dispute, and it was agreed that the capital would not be a part of any state. The current site of the capital city on the banks of the Potomac River was chosen and declared to be the District of Columbia. New York had been the nation's first capital, but until the new capital was ready, the title moved to Philadelphia as part of the compromise. Construction of the White House began in Washington in 1792, with work on the Capitol starting the following year.

26. **Answer: D. Yorktown.** On October 19, 1781, Yorktown was the last significant battle of the war and one that the Continental Army probably would not have won without help from France. Roughly 9,000 French soldiers and 15,000 French sailors joined about 11,000 Americans to surround a much smaller British and Hessian force. General Charles Cornwallis's loss broke Britain's will to continue fighting, and the English Crown entered negotiations to end the war. It took nearly two years before the Treaty of Paris was signed, which marked the official cessation of hostilities.

Explorers and Adventurers

★ ★

Since North America first became known, pioneers and explorers have blazed new trails and pushed the boundaries a little bit farther on land, in the seas, and through the skies. Their travels into uncharted territories have led to new American frontiers.

1. Christopher Columbus is famous for "discovering" America, but was he the first European to journey to the new continent? True or False: Almost 500 years before Columbus sailed the ocean blue, Vikings not only landed, but also settled in North America.

2. Robert Peary wasn't alone when he discovered the North Pole in 1909. Peary's codiscoverer was finally recognized with a joint medal by Congress on January 28, 1944. Who was he?

A. Matthew Henson
B. Matthew Perry
C. James Cook
D. Richard Byrd

3. Everyone is familiar with Neil Armstrong's first words as he stepped onto the surface of the moon: "That's one small step for man, one giant leap for mankind." But what was the second sentence uttered from the lunar surface?

A. "It sure is good to stretch."
B. "Beautiful, beautiful. Magnificent desolation."
C. "Here comes Buzz now."
D. "The surface is fine and powdery."

Answers

★ ★ ★ ★ ★ ★

1. Answer: True. Around 1005 Thorfinn and Gudrid Karlsefni led a group of homesteaders that numbered between 65 and 265. They came with livestock and supplies to settle what they called "Vineland," and they stayed for two years until conflicts with the native people caused them to leave. Although the exact sites of these settlements are unknown, many historians believe they were in the northeastern areas of the continent. Some archaeologists also believe the Norse explored as far down the coast as North Carolina.

2. Answer: A. Matthew Henson. Following the discovery of the North Pole, Henson, an African American, was often dismissed as Robert Peary's servant, but Peary considered him a colleague and codiscoverer of the pole. Henson was belatedly acknowledged in 1944. Along with Peary and Henson at the pole were four Inuit guides, men and women, who kept the entire expedition on track.

3. Answer: D. "The surface is fine and powdery." After his famous first words on the moon, Neil Armstrong simply described what he saw there. The second man on the moon, Buzz Aldrin, said, "Beautiful, beautiful. Magnificent desolation." Apollo 12 astronaut Pete Conrad, whose height was the shortest in the astronaut corps, jumped down from his lunar module and said, "Whoopie! That may have been a small one for Neil, but it's a long one for me."

Questions

★ ★ ★ ★ ★ ★ ★

4. One of the earliest explorers of the western coast of North American was Francisco de Ulloa, and it is in accounts of his exploits that the name "California" first appears in relation to the peninsula we know today as Baja California. What do scholars believe is the origin of the name California?

A. It was the name of Ulloa's navigator.
B. It came from a work of fiction.
C. It is old Spanish for "coastal."
D. It is derived from the Native American name for the region.

5. What was the name of the ship or ships that brought colonists to the first permanent British settlement in North America?

A. The *Nina*, the *Pinta*, and the *Santa Maria*
B. The *Mayflower*
C. The *Susan Constant*, the *Discovery*, and the *Godspeed*
D. The *Half Moon*

6. Only one person has ever won the Medal of Honor, the Pulitzer prize, and the Service Cross of the German Eagle. Who is it?

A. Amelia Earhart
B. Charles Lindbergh
C. Douglas "Wrong Way" Corrigan
D. Merriweather Lewis

ANSWERS

★ ★ ★ ★ ★ ★ ★

4. Answer: B. It came from a work of fiction. An early 16th-century work of fiction, *Las Sergas de Esplandian* by Ordonez de Montalvo, tells the story of a force of Amazons led by Queen Calafia of the island of California. The island was described as being near the Terrestrial Paradise, an island overflowing with gold. Many early Spanish explorers came to the New World in search of such a paradise, and for a short time they thought they may have found it in California.

5. Answer: C. The *Susan Constant*, the *Discovery*, and the *Godspeed*. The first permanent British settlement in North America was founded in Jamestown, Virginia, on May 14, 1607, by the passengers of these ships. In 1619 the colony established the first representative government on the continent. It also brought the first African slaves to the colonies and built the first Anglican church. A previous British settlement that was intended to be permanent was established in 1587 on Roanoke Island on the coast of what is now North Carolina. By 1590, it had disappeared with virtually no trace. The mystery of this disappearance continues to this day.

6. Answer: B. Charles Lindbergh. Aviator Lindbergh won the Medal of Honor for performing the first solo nonstop flight from New York to Paris in 1927. The Germans were also impressed with him, and in 1938 Hermann Goering awarded the Service Cross of the German Eagle to Lindbergh, the only U.S. citizen to receive that honor. In 1954, Lindbergh's account of his famous flight, *The Spirit of St. Louis,* won him a Pulitzer prize.

QUESTIONS

★ ★ ★ ★ ★ ★ ★

7. Reporter Elizabeth Cochrane may be best known for her 1889 attempt to beat the hero of Jules Verne's novel and travel around the world in less than 80 days. But Cochrane used a pen name, which she borrowed from a song by Stephen Foster. What was it?

A. Susannah Louisiana
B. Sweet Adeline
C. Jeannie Brown
D. Nellie Bly

8. Early European explorers of the American West sometimes brought artists with them to chronicle their journeys. One such artist, who was among the first European pioneers to set foot on the floor of the Grand Canyon, supplied drawings and written accounts of the trip. He went on to be a prolific writer. Who was he?

A. Thomas Nuttall
B. Mark Twain
C. Heinrich Mollhausen
D. John Greenleaf Whittier

9. Each year the people of Ocean Shores, Washington, gather to celebrate "Undiscovery Day." They have a party and finish the evening by wading out into the ocean and shouting, "Hey, George!" Who are they shouting for?

A. George Washington
B. George Vancouver
C. George Tacoma
D. King George III

ANSWERS

★ ★ ★ ★ ★ ★

7. **Answer: D. Nellie Bly.** Cochrane adopted the name Nellie Bly as a writer at the *Pittsburgh Dispatch*, and she went on to fame as an undercover reporter at the New York *World*. Her exposé on the asylum on Blackwell's Island brought about reforms for the mentally ill. And she beat Phileas Fogg in her round-the-world trip. Her time: 72 days, 6 hours, 11 minutes, and 14 seconds.

8. **Answer: C. Heinrich Mollhausen.** Mollhausen took part in Lieutenant Amiel Weeks Whipple's Army exhibition in search of a railroad route to the Pacific in 1853, as well as Lieutenant Joseph Christmas Ives's expedition up the Colorado River. He became one of the most well-known writers of 19th-century Germany with 45 novels and 80 short stories, most of which dealt with the American West. Germans knew him as "the old trapper," but his works are rarely read today.

9. **Answer: B. George Vancouver.** Vancouver surveyed the West Coast in 1791. He sailed more than 30,000 miles and charted more than 4,000 miles of coastline from California to Alaska. He named Mount Baker, Mount Rainier, Port Orchard, and Puget Sound, and his own name graces cities in Washington state and British Columbia, Canada, as well as a Canadian island. He did not, however, discover Ocean Shores, Washington.

Questions

★ ★ ★ ★ ★ ★ ★ ★

10. The final Apollo lunar module, from the Apollo 17 mission, bears a plaque reading: "Here man completed his first explorations of the moon. May the spirit of peace in which we came be reflected in the lives of all mankind." It was to have had a different second sentence, but it was changed by NASA officials just weeks before the launch. What did it originally say?

A. "We will come again in peace for all mankind."
B. "God bless America."
C. "One small step for a man, one giant leap for mankind."
D. It was to list the names of all the Apollo astronauts.

11. This mountain, originally named "James' Peak" for the first man to scale it successfully, had its name changed to honor a man who failed to scale it. What is the new name of the mountain?

A. Mount Rainier
B. Mount Vernon
C. Pikes Peak
D. Mount McKinley

12. On February 26, 1955, George Franklin Smith of Manhattan Beach, California, became the first to perform a particular feat. What did he do?

A. Break the sound barrier
B. Go up in a test rocket
C. Walk on the floor of the Atlantic Ocean
D. Bail out of an airplane flying at supersonic speed

43

Answers

★ ★ ★ ★ ★ ★

10. **Answer: A. "We will come again in peace for all mankind."** There were 20 Apollo missions planned, but due to budget cuts, Apollos 18–20 were grounded. Officials at NASA decided at the last minute that it might not be a good idea to promise to return to the moon.

11. **Answer: C. Pikes Peak.** In 1806 an army unit led by Zebulon Montgomery Pike spotted a towering mountain that, Pike said, "appeared like a small blue cloud." It took more than a week for the soldiers to reach the mountain's foothills. The conditions of the climb were punishing, the temperature was −4 degrees Fahrenheit, and the soldiers turned back. Fourteen years later, the summit was finally reached by Dr. Edwin James and his group and was named in his honor. In the 1830s, however, people began calling it Pikes Peak. The name stuck, and by the 1850s it had been officially changed.

12. **Answer: D. Bail out of an airplane flying at supersonic speed.** George Franklin Smith was at an altitude of 6,500 feet and flying at 777 miles per hour when his seat automatically detached itself from his F-100A Super Sabre Jet fighter. His clothes were cut to shreds, and his helmet, his oxygen mask, and even his socks flew off. He felt the push of his organs, which, under the G force he was experiencing, weighed 40 times more than normal. He landed in the ocean where he was rescued, but he spent the next six months in the hospital.

QUESTIONS

★ ★ ★ ★ ★ ★ ★

13. Christopher Columbus made four trips across the Atlantic Ocean to the New World. His explorations set off a flood of Europeans traveling to the Americas for exploration and settlement. True or False: Columbus never stepped foot on the mainland of North America.

14. In 1910 she became the first woman in America, and the second in the world, to earn a pilot's license. She was also the first woman to fly successfully across the English Channel. Who was she?

A. Amelia Earhart
B. Harriet Quimby
C. Clara Barton
D. Jenny Lind

15. When the *Titanic* sank in 1912, it was lost to the world for more than 70 years. Expeditions from around the world searched for the wreckage in the North Atlantic, but it remained elusive until discovered by an American undersea explorer. Who was that explorer?

A. Robert Ballard
B. James Cameron
C. Graham Hawkes
D. Jacques Cousteau

Answers

★ ★ ★ ★ ★ ★

13. **Answer: True.** Christopher Columbus and company never made it past the Caribbean. During his famous 1492 trip, Columbus reached the Bahamas, but he returned home to tell everyone he'd found the outer islands of China. The credit for "discovering" the North American mainland goes to Spanish adventurer Juan Ponce de Leon, who, in his search for the Fountain of Youth, found his way to the Florida coastline.

14. **Answer: B. Harriet Quimby.** Journalist Quimby became fascinated with airplanes after covering an air show in 1910. She set off to cross the English Channel in a biplane on April 16, 1912, and succeeded in her quest. Unfortunately, she failed to make headlines for her feat due to a tragedy—the sinking of the *Titanic*—that occupied everyone's minds. She died in July of that year behind the controls of her plane as she tried to set a new world speed record. She was 37.

15. **Answer: A. Robert Ballard.** In 1985, Ballard was on a U.S. Navy mission to hunt down a nuclear submarine lost during the Cold War. He was also interested in the *Titanic*, so he made sure his exploration took him close to the region where the ocean liner was thought to be. Other expeditions led by Ballard located historic sunken battleships, such as the U.S.S. *Yorktown* at the Midway Islands, as well as Black Sea relics that may have belonged to a civilization buried by a catastrophic flood.

QUESTIONS

★ ★ ★ ★ ★ ★ ★

16. English sea captain James Cook came within 70 miles of this site in 1774, but it was an American, John Davis, who first landed there. Where did Davis come ashore?

A. Australia
B. Hong Kong
C. Antarctica
D. Hawaii

17. In 1524 Florentine navigator Giovanni da Verrazano was the first European to discover what is now New York Harbor and its river, but another explorer was the first European to travel up the river and look around. Who was he?

A. Peter Minuit
B. Henry Hudson
C. John Smith
D. Peter Stuyvesant

18. True or False: By 1492, when Christopher Columbus set out toward North America, most Europeans knew the world was round.

19. Americans began manned missions into space in the early 1960s, but the entire rocket (except the capsule) would be destroyed during the mission. For a number of years, NASA tried to develop a craft that could make multiple return missions into space, a goal they finally attained with the launch of the first space shuttle on April 12, 1981. What was the name of this shuttle?

A. *Columbia*
B. *Challenger*
C. *Discovery*
D. *Endeavor*

ANSWERS

★ ★ ★ ★ ★ ★ ★

16. **Answer: C. Antarctica.** John Davis had been looking for seals in the South Shetland Islands when he set foot on the Antarctic peninsula in 1821. The continent of Antarctica is the coldest place on Earth. It receives so little precipitation—two inches a year, the same as the Sahara Desert—that it technically qualifies as a desert.

17. **Answer: B. Henry Hudson.** Hudson was looking for a northeast passage to China in 1609 but instead discovered the route to Albany, New York. The Hudson River now bears his name.

18. **Answer: True.** The idea that Christopher Columbus was the first European to realize the world was not flat only dates back to Washington Irving's 1828 biography of the navigator. Irving probably knew the tale was fictional but put it in to add color.

19. **Answer: A. *Columbia*.** The shuttle that flew the first five shuttle missions was named after a 1792 Boston sloop, the first to navigate the northwestern river that also took its name. Robert Gray, the sloop's captain, also led the sloop *Columbia* on the first American circumnavigation of the globe. Other famous vessels named *Columbia* include the first U.S. Naval ship to circle the globe and the command module of the Apollo 11 mission.

Presidential Trivia

The president of the United States is often referred to as "the leader of the free world." It's a serious position and one with a lot of responsibility. Only 42 men in the history of the world have held it. Much has been said about presidents like Washington, Lincoln, and Kennedy—but how much do you know about some of the other presidents like Harrison, Taft, or Wilson? Let's find out.

1. Which state holds the honor of being the birthplace of the most U.S. presidents?

A. Virginia
B. Ohio
C. New York
D. Massachusetts

2. Which first lady met her future husband while they were both acting in a local theater group?

A. Pat Nixon
B. Eleanor Roosevelt
C. Nancy Reagan
D. Mary Todd Lincoln

3. Obviously when the United States achieved its independence from Britain, the first few presidents would have to have been British subjects at some time in their lives. Who was the first U.S. president who was not born a British citizen?

A. Andrew Jackson
B. James Madison
C. Martin Van Buren
D. John Quincy Adams

ANSWERS

★ ★ ★ ★ ★ ★ ★

1. **Answer: A. Virginia.** Virginia has been the motherland for eight future executives-in-chief, including George Washington, Thomas Jefferson, and James Madison. Ohio, the "Buckeye State," is runner-up with seven presidents-to-be, but it is tops in a different way: It is the only state to birth three successive presidents (Ulysses S. Grant, Rutherford B. Hayes, and James Garfield).

2. **Answer: A. Pat Nixon.** Her real name was Thelma Catherine, but her dad quickly nicknamed her after her birth on March 16, calling her his "Saint Patrick's babe in the morn." She and Richard Nixon, then a young lawyer, became acquainted when they both auditioned for the same amateur play. It is said that Nixon proposed after the first rehearsal and, when she rebuffed his advances, he even offered to drive her to and from dates with other boys. Eventually, he won her over, and they married in 1940.

3. **Answer: C. Martin Van Buren.** Every president has been born in North America, but eight of the first nine presidents entered the world while the Union Jack still flew overhead. Van Buren was born after the Revolution in Kinderhook, New York, on December 5, 1782. His hometown also led to the acceptance of a new word in the American lexicon. Van Buren was often called "Old Kinderhook," which was shortened to "OK" and used as a slogan by the Democratic party.

Questions

★ ★ ★ ★ ★ ★

4. True or False: One of the selected members of the Warren Commission to investigate the assassination of John F. Kennedy had once been fired by Kennedy.

5. If the president and vice-president are both incapable of carrying out the duties of office, what political position is next in line to succeed them?

A. Speaker of the House of Representatives
B. President pro tempore of the Senate
C. Attorney general
D. Secretary of state

6. In the presidential election of 1840, the campaign cry went up for "Tippecanoe and Tyler, Too." Who was "Tippecanoe"?

A. Terrence Tippecanoe
B. Henry Clay
C. William Henry Harrison
D. John Tyler

Answers

★ ★ ★ ★ ★ ★

4. Answer: True. Allen Dulles, a member of the 1963 commission, had been the Director of the Central Intelligence Agency (CIA) since 1953 and the days of President Dwight D. Eisenhower. He maintained his role with the CIA during the first year of the Kennedy Administration, but Kennedy fired him in 1961 following the bungled Cuban invasion known as the Bay of Pigs. An internal CIA audit of the operation, kept secret until 1998, blamed the failure on a series of mistakes made by the agency in the planning and execution of the invasion.

5. Answer: A. Speaker of the House of Representatives. The order of presidential succession has changed several times since it was first spelled out in Article II of the Constitution (which gave Congress the power to pick a temporary replacement). The most recent elaboration was the Presidential Succession Act of 1947, which set the line of succession to move, after the vice-president, to the speaker of the house, the president pro tempore of the Senate, and then to each secretary of the cabinet, in the order their departments were created.

6. Answer: C. William Henry Harrison. Harrison, a military hero, was the Whig Party's 1840 presidential candidate. He was nicknamed "Old Tippecanoe" for his victory over Native American forces at the Battle of Tippecanoe in 1811. Harrison's appeal was largely to the North, so John Tyler, a Virginian, was placed on the ticket to please the South. The Whigs won, and Harrison was inaugurated in March 1841.

Questions

★ ★ ★ ★ ★ ★ ★

7. Andrew Johnson was Abraham Lincoln's vice-president after the election of 1864, and after Lincoln's assassination, Johnson stepped into the presidency. Who was Johnson's vice-president?

A. Ulysses S. Grant
B. William Seward
C. Hannibal Hamlin
D. No one

8. Who is the only U.S. president to have written a Pulitzer-prize-winning book?

A. Franklin D. Roosevelt
B. Woodrow Wilson
C. Jimmy Carter
D. John F. Kennedy

9. We often assume that presidential scandals are recent phenomena, but they have been a part of presidential life since the earliest days of the nation. One of the most famous presidential scandals, Teapot Dome, involved the administration of Warren G. Harding. What commodity was at the center of this scandal?

A. Tea
B. Munitions
C. Silver
D. Oil

Answers

★ ★ ★ ★ ★ ★

7. **Answer: D. No one.** There was no law in place to name a new vice-president if the current one became president. Andrew Johnson was a Democrat who had been drafted to run with Abraham Lincoln by the Republicans, who wanted to demonstrate a bipartisan spirit in the midst of the Civil War. Later, Johnson was one vote away from impeachment for attempting to dismiss his secretary of war. Such a dismissal required the approval of the Senate, and Johnson had never asked for it.

8. **Answer: D. John F. Kennedy.** While recuperating in a hospital after spinal surgery, then-Senator Kennedy wrote a collection of accounts describing decisive moments in the lives of famous politicians such as John Quincy Adams, Daniel Webster, and Sam Houston. The book, *Profiles in Courage*, was published in 1956 and won the Pulitzer the following year. Even though Kennedy's image exuded youth and vitality, he was in poor health for much of his adult life. At least four times as an adult, Kennedy was administered last rites.

9. **Answer: D. Oil.** The scandal revolved around Albert B. Fall, Warren G. Harding's secretary of the interior, who secretly leased to a private company tracts of land that had been set aside as naval oil reserves. Fall became the first-ever cabinet member convicted of a criminal offense, and a number of other Washington officials were implicated. The land in question, Teapot Dome near Casper, Wyoming, got its name from a rock in the oil reserve that looked like a teapot.

Questions

★ ★ ★ ★ ★ ★ ★

10. George H. W. Bush and George W. Bush are America's second father and son to serve as president. Who was the first father-and-son pair?

A. Andrew Johnson and Lyndon Johnson
B. Teddy Roosevelt and Franklin Roosevelt
C. William Henry Harrison and Benjamin Harrison
D. John Adams and John Quincy Adams

11. On September 23, 1952, Richard Nixon delivered a famous speech in which he referred to his cocker spaniel. What was the dog's name?

A. Buddy
B. Checkers
C. Fala
D. Millie

12. What does Harry Truman's middle initial, *S*, stand for?

A. Samuel
B. Simpson
C. Seeburg
D. Nothing

Answers

★ ★ ★ ★ ★ ★

10. **Answer: D. John Adams and John Quincy Adams.** The sixth president was the son of the second. Andrew Johnson, the 17th president, was not related to Lyndon Johnson, the 36th president, at all. Teddy Roosevelt, president number 26, and Franklin Roosevelt, number 32, were distant cousins, although Teddy was actually the uncle of Franklin's wife Eleanor. William Henry Harrison, the 9th president, was the grandfather of Benjamin Harrison, the 23rd.

11. **Answer: B. Checkers.** Long before Watergate became a household word, Richard Nixon was caught up in another scandal. As a vice-presidential candidate, the then-senator went on prime-time television to defend himself against charges that he had received secret contributions from backers. As part of the emotional speech, he told America that Checkers had been sent to his family as a gift, but he insisted, "Regardless of what they say about it, we're going to keep it." By the way, all the other names belonged to presidential pooches, too. Buddy was Bill Clinton's chocolate Lab; Fala was FDR's terrier; and Millie was the springer spaniel of George H. W. Bush.

12. **Answer: D. Nothing.** Harry Truman's folks, Martha Ellen and John, did not give their firstborn son a middle name. But apparently two of the Truman's relatives had names that started with *S*, so they attached the single letter between their son's first and last names as an honor to them.

Questions

★ ★ ★ ★ ★ ★ ★

13. Presidents like to put names to their policies. Over the years we've seen the *Monroe Doctrine*, Franklin Roosevelt's *New Deal*, and Kennedy's *New Frontier*. Which of the following terms did Lyndon Johnson use to describe his domestic policy?

A. *The Great Society*
B. *The Fair Deal*
C. *War for Prosperity*
D. *Hippie Revolution*

14. Most presidents have held other government positions before and after their time in office. Who is the only U.S. president to become Chief Justice of the U.S. Supreme Court?

A. James Buchanan
B. Millard Fillmore
C. William Howard Taft
D. James Monroe

15. Who was president when the 50th state entered the Union?

A. Franklin Roosevelt
B. Harry Truman
C. Dwight Eisenhower
D. John F. Kennedy

Answers

★ ★ ★ ★ ★ ★ ★

13. **Answer: A. *The Great Society.*** In his 1965 State of the Union speech, Lyndon Johnson expanded on the War on Poverty idea that he had unveiled the previous year. His Great Society plan called for a number of federally sponsored programs that could improve the average American's quality of life and shrink racial divisions. During his administration, Congress passed several civil-rights and education acts. The Great Society also saw Congress create the Jobs Corps, Operation Head Start, Medicare, and Medicaid.

14. **Answer: C. William Howard Taft.** Taft, who served as president from 1909 until 1913, was appointed Chief Justice in 1921 by Warren G. Harding and served on the court for nearly nine years. It was during the conservative Taft's stewardship that construction on a new, more suitable Supreme Court building began—the justices had previously met mostly in the basement of the Capitol. During the 19th century, they sometimes even met in Washington taverns. By the way, Taft was also the largest president, tipping the scales at a hefty 300-plus pounds.

15. **Answer: C. Dwight Eisenhower.** Eisenhower was the country's chief executive when both Alaska (the 49th state) and Hawaii (50th) were admitted. He endorsed the admission of both territories as early as his "I Like Ike" campaign in 1952, but disagreements with Congress stalled necessary legislation until 1958. Hawaii became a state on August 21, 1959.

QUESTIONS

★ ★ ★ ★ ★ ★ ★

16. True or False: The Hoover vacuum cleaner is named after Herbert Hoover.

17. Which future president was born William Jefferson Blythe IV?

A. William Howard Taft
B. William McKinley
C. Bill Clinton
D. Thomas Jefferson

18. One of the early presidents lived in an estate called Monticello. On which U.S. cash denomination does Monticello appear?

A. Nickel
B. $5 bill
C. $50 bill
D. $500 bill

19. Which president was known as the "silent president"?

A. Woodrow Wilson
B. Grover Cleveland
C. James Madison
D. Calvin Coolidge

Answers

★ ★ ★ ★ ★ ★

16. **Answer: False.** Herbert Hoover was a successful engineer, but the machine, initially called a "suction sweeper," takes its name from the man who first marketed the labor-saving device in 1908, W. H. "Boss" Hoover. A few other things have been named after the 31st president, however: Hoover Dam, the Hooverville shantytowns of the Great Depression, and the asteroid Hooveria.

17. **Answer: C. Bill Clinton.** His father, for whom he was named, died in a car accident before the future president was born. Clinton's mother, Virginia Kelley, later married Roger Clinton, and young Bill adopted his stepfather's surname.

18. **Answer: A. Nickel.** Monticello, which was Thomas Jefferson's Virginia home, also appears on the backside of certain $2 bills. The Roman neoclassical structure is the only house in the United States on the United Nations' prestigious World Heritage List of sites that must be protected at all costs.

19. **Answer: D. Calvin Coolidge.** "Silent Cal" Coolidge was known as one of the most laconic presidents. He slept late, took two-hour naps each day, and went to bed early. It is said that at one dinner party a young woman sitting next to Coolidge confided that she had bet she could get more than three words out of him. His reply: "You lose." Still, he was very popular during his term for his frugal ways at a time when Americans were spending money lavishly.

QUESTIONS

★ ★ ★ ★ ★ ★ ★

20. True or false: John F. Kennedy was the youngest person who ever served as the president of the United States.

21. Lyndon Johnson was an audacious man. His larger-than-life Texas ways often got him into trouble with Washington insiders. What did Johnson do on October 20, 1965, that sent much of the world's press corps into overtime?

A. Lifted his shirt for photographers
B. Belched during a press conference
C. Ignored a repeated question from a reporter
D. Slapped a nosy TV interviewer

22. What U.S. president's portrait appears on the $100,000 bill?

A. James Madison
B. Woodrow Wilson
C. Grover Cleveland
D. William McKinley

Answers

★ ★ ★ ★ ★ ★

20. **Answer: False.** At age 43, John F. Kennedy was the youngest person to be elected president, but Theodore Roosevelt was a little more than 42 years and 10 months old when he took the oath of office on September 14, 1901. He had been vice-president and became president after William McKinley was assassinated at the Pan-American Exposition in Buffalo, New York.

21. **Answer: A. Lifted his shirt for photographers.** Twelve days after gallbladder surgery, LBJ was asked by the White House press how he was feeling. Figuring one picture was worth at least a thousand words, he lifted the tails of his shirt and revealed the 12-inch scar that grossly crossed his stomach. His lack of decorum made front-page news all over the world.

22. **Answer: B. Woodrow Wilson.** Yes, Virginia, there really are $100,000 bills. But these Gold Certificate bills, printed in 1934, have never been placed in general circulation—they are used for transactions between the Federal Reserve System and the Treasury Department. Since Wilson established the Federal Reserve System during his presidency, it was only fitting that his portrait appear on the bill. All four presidents listed *do* appear on various denominations of U.S. currency—James Madison is on the $5,000 bill, Grover Cleveland is on the $1,000 bill, and William McKinley shows up on the $500 bill.

Questions

★ ★ ★ ★ ★ ★ ★

23. The coat of arms on the presidential seal features an eagle holding an olive branch in its right talon. What is the eagle holding in its left talon?

A. A scroll
B. A musket
C. A flag
D. Arrows

24. Some presidents have had their terms shortened through illness or assassination. Which U.S. president served the shortest term?

A. Zachary Taylor
B. William Henry Harrison
C. James Garfield
D. John F. Kennedy

25. In 1937, the date for the presidential inauguration was set at January 20. Before that year, on what date had the inauguration been held?

A. March 4
B. January 1
C. November 10
D. February 14

ANSWERS

★ ★ ★ ★ ★ ★

23. **Answer: D. Arrows.** The eagle is grasping 13 arrows in its claw. Its head was originally turned to them, but President Harry Truman had the seal redesigned to make the eagle face right, the heraldic direction of honor, toward the olive branch of peace. The seal is similar to the "Great Seal of the United States," which was designed by William Barton and approved by Congress in 1782.

24. **Answer: B. William Henry Harrison.** Harrison was inaugurated on a cold, stormy March 4, 1841. His age, 67 during the campaign, had been an election issue, so to demonstrate his youthful vitality, he refused to wear a hat or coat as he rode to the Capitol on a white horse. After the oath of office, he gave the longest inaugural address on record (a whopping 8,578 words delivered in about an hour and forty-five minutes). The common wisdom is that Harrison died of a cold he caught that day, but this is not true. His death was due to pneumonia, which is caused by a virus, not cold weather. In fact, he didn't report feeling ill until March 27. He was diagnosed with pneumonia the next day, and he died on April 4.

25. **Answer: A. March 4.** The 20th Amendment to the Constitution, known as the "lame duck amendment," moved the date to the earlier January 20. Technological advancements in transportation and communication made it unnecessary to have as long a period of transition as had been in place. Congress proposed the change in 1932, and it was ratified by the states on January 23, 1933, but the new date didn't take practical effect until FDR's second inauguration in 1937.

QUESTIONS

★ ★ ★ ★ ★ ★ ★

26. At some points during American history, it has not been completely clear what was happening in the White House until years afterword. Although the public remained unaware, one president suffered a debilitating stroke while in office. Which first lady is said to have made most of her husband's decisions during this time?

A. Eleanor Roosevelt
B. Dolley Madison
C. Edith Wilson
D. Mamie Eisenhower

27. Which president initiated the first Easter Monday Egg Roll at the White House?

A. Rutherford B. Hayes
B. Andrew Jackson
C. James Monroe
D. William McKinley

28. Franklin Roosevelt's New Deal introduced a number of government programs to help lift the United States out of the Great Depression. Most of the programs were known by their initials. Which one of these was *not* a part of the New Deal?

A. TVA
B. FRC
C. WPA
D. FDIC

Answers

★ ★ ★ ★ ★ ★

26. **Answer: C. Edith Wilson.** Woodrow Wilson married Edith Bolling Galt in December 1915, less than two years after his first first lady passed away. But when the president suffered a paralytic attack in 1919, the new Mrs. Wilson apparently handled more than just the White House's social activities. Mrs. Wilson sequestered her husband during his illness and, while she claimed his brain was "clear and untouched," she replaced sitting cabinet members with Wilson loyalists and often signed his name to veto messages and legislation.

27. **Answer: A. Rutherford B. Hayes.** The original site of the Washington Easter Egg Roll was the U.S. Capitol grounds. But Members of Congress got tired of walking through broken eggshells and torn-up lawns, so some spring Scrooges passed a law in 1876 forbidding the use of the Capitol area as a children's playground. There are several versions of what happened next, but one story says that President Hayes, taking a walk on Easter Sunday, was asked by some kids if they could use the White House lawn for the event. The rest, as they say, is history.

28. **Answer: B. FRC.** The Federal Radio Commission, forerunner of the Federal Communications Commission, was created in 1927 under President Calvin Coolidge. The TVA (Tennessee Valley Authority) brought electric power and flood control for much of the southeastern United States. The WPA (Work Projects Administration) created a federalized work-relief program. The FDIC (Federal Deposit Insurance Corporation) insured the nation's banks.

Questions

★ ★ ★ ★ ★ ★ ★

29. Four U.S. Presidents have been assassinated while in office. Which one of these lived the longest before succumbing to his injuries?

A. Abraham Lincoln
B. James Garfield
C. William McKinley
D. John F. Kennedy

30. The amount of the president's salary is always available to the public, but we don't often pay a lot of attention to it. It's interesting to see how it has fluctuated through the years. What was the annual presidential salary of Harry S. Truman?

A. $50,000
B. $25,000
C. $75,000
D. $100,000

31. Many first ladies are as famous as their husbands, but not every president enters the White House with a first lady. Who was the first president to be married in the White House?

A. John Tyler
B. Grover Cleveland
C. Teddy Roosevelt
D. Calvin Coolidge

Answers

★ ★ ★ ★ ★ ★ ★

29. **Answer: B. James Garfield.** Abraham Lincoln was shot in the evening and passed away the following morning. William McKinley was shot and successfully operated on, but he died of gangrene infection eight days later. John F. Kennedy was pronounced dead half an hour after being struck by gunshots in Dallas's Dealey Plaza. But Garfield lingered for more than 11 weeks before dying of his gunshot wounds.

30. **Answer: D. $100,000.** Set by Congress, the presidential salary was originally $25,000. It increased to $50,000 in 1873, and an additional stipend of $25,000 was added in 1907. The salary itself was again increased to $75,000 in 1909 and, during Harry S. Truman's presidency, the salary was bumped to $100,000. The stipend was also increased to $90,000. In 1969, the yearly presidential salary was raised to $200,000, with an additional $100,000 earmarked for travel and $50,000 for expenses. In 2001, the annual presidential salary was doubled again to $400,000.

31. **Answer: B. Grover Cleveland.** The 49-year-old Cleveland held the ceremonies in the White House slightly more than a year after his inauguration in 1885. He married Frances Folsom, the daughter of a former law partner. They went on to have three daughters and two sons. John Tyler's first wife died almost a year and a half into his term as president, and he remarried almost two years later, becoming the first president to marry while in office. The wedding itself, however, took place in New York rather than the White House.

The Great Depression

★ ★ ★ ★ ★ ★ ★ ★ ★ ★ ★ ★ ★ ★ ★ ★ ★

It was a period of time in American history like no other. The economy seemed to be in ruins, and, with the Dust Bowl, agriculture didn't seem any better. If the Roaring '20s were America's wild party, the Depression of the '30s was America's hangover. Yet it was a formative time for those who lived through it—it defined a generation. What do you know about the highs and lows of the Great Depression?

1. The stock market crash on October 29, 1929, ushered in the Great Depression. On what day of the week did this happen?

A. Monday
B. Tuesday
C. Thursday
D. Friday

2. True or False: The suicide rate among investors reached an unprecedented high just after October 24, 1929, the first time the market crashed in that year.

3. Early in 1929, John Jacob Raskob, chief executive of General Motors, published an article in *Ladies Home Journal*. What was its title?

A. "The Prosperity to Come"
B. "An Economic Crash Is Coming"
C. "Buy More Cars"
D. "Everybody Ought to Be Rich"

Answers

★ ★ ★ ★ ★ ★

1. Answer: B. Tuesday. The day is commonly known as "Black Tuesday," and the market lost more than $10 billion in just a few hours. There was a "Black Thursday" the previous week, when 13 million shares were sold off, but Wall Street bankers tried to inspire confidence in the market by propping up stock prices over the next couple of days with a cash infusion of millions of dollars. Obviously, their attempts failed. The more recent October 19, 1987, crash was called "Black Monday."

2. Answer: False. Contrary to popular belief, the suicide rate among investors was actually higher in the period before Black Thursday.

3. Answer: D. "Everybody Ought to Be Rich." John Jacob Raskob's article argued that if every American invested just $15 a week in common stocks they could all become rich. There was a major glitch in his plan even before the stock market crashed—the average American worker only earned about $17–$22 a week at the time. The article highlights the "psychology of prosperity" of the Roaring '20s, which was about to take a serious hit.

QUESTIONS

★ ★ ★ ★ ★ ★ ★

4. It was Herbert Hoover who dubbed the economic downturn of the '30s a "depression." Two previous economic crises in 1873 and 1893 had been labeled with a different name. What was it?

A. Recession
B. Panic
C. Collapse
D. Shut Down

5. This bank robber, celebrated as a 20th-century Robin Hood in a song by Woody Guthrie, so hated his nickname that he killed at least two people for using it. Who was this gangster and his nickname?

A. Charles "Pretty Boy" Floyd
B. Benjamin "Bugsy" Siegel
C. George "Machine Gun" Kelly
D. Lester "Baby Face" Nelson

6. In 1931, author Edward Angly published a book with the title *Oh Yeah?* What did this book contain?

A. A denial that the country was in a depression
B. A collection of optimistic predictions by Herbert Hoover
C. A proposal for ending the Depression
D. Recipes that cost 25 cents or less

7. During the Great Depression "hobo nickels" were often traded for food and clothing. What were hobo nickels?

A. Cigarettes
B. Wooden nickels
C. Tall tales or stories
D. Nickels with altered faces

Answers

★ ★ ★ ★ ★ ★ ★

4. Answer: B. Panic. Even though similar economic downturns had been called "panics," Herbert Hoover did not want to "panic" the American people, so he selected a different word to refer to the situation. His term "depression" stuck.

5. Answer: A. Charles "Pretty Boy" Floyd. During the Depression, a hatred of banks (which often foreclosed on Midwestern farmers) existed among the public, and bank robber Charles Arthur Floyd became a folk hero to some. He hated being called "Pretty Boy," a nickname first given to him by prostitutes at the houses of ill repute he'd been known to visit. When he was shot down by federal agents in 1934, his dying words were "I'm Charles Arthur Floyd!"

6. Answer: B. A collection of optimistic predictions by Herbert Hoover. After the stock market crash, Hoover and his cabinet members tried to instill confidence by making hopeful statements about the economy. Knowing an opportunity when he saw it, Edward Angly published his collection of those statements under the sarcastic title.

7. Answer: D. Nickels with altered faces. Hobo nickels were a unique form of Depression folk art. Nickels during the '30s had a portrait of a Native American on their face. Impoverished artists would use a knife and chisel to rework that portrait, often carving a famous person, a clown, or another recognizable face in its place. George Washington "Bo" Hughes was one of the most prolific hobo nickel artists.

QUESTIONS

★ ★ ★ ★ ★ ★ ★

8. In the years of the Great Depression, people often turned to entertainment to take their minds off their problems. What song from a Walt Disney cartoon became a surprise hit?

A. "Who's Afraid of the Big Bad Wolf?"
B. "I Won't Grow Up"
C. "I've Got No Strings"
D. "When You Wish Upon a Star"

9. In 1932 a group called the "Bonus Army" or "Bonus Expeditionary Force" converged on Washington, D.C. What did they demand?

A. Immediate bonus payments for their service in World War I
B. Bonuses for the nation's factory employees
C. Extra incentives for Americans to buy stocks
D. More time to pay their taxes

10. This Depression-era novelist was known for such works as *Tobacco Road,* which depicted the lives of poor, rural Southerners. Who was this novelist?

A. William Faulkner
B. Erskine Caldwell
C. John Steinbeck
D. William Saroyan

ANSWERS

★ ★ ★ ★ ★ ★

8. Answer: A. "Who's Afraid of the Big Bad Wolf?" Walt Disney's *Three Little Pigs* opened at New York's Radio City Music Hall in May 1933, and its catchy tune about fear struck a chord during the tough times. Even President Franklin Roosevelt said the movie was one of his favorites. Radio stations and bands wanted to play the song, but Disney hadn't even arranged to publish the music. To meet demands for sheet music, Disney sent musicians with flashlights into darkened theaters to copy down words and music by listening to the soundtrack.

9. Answer: A. Immediate bonus payments for their service in World War I. In 1924 Congress had voted for such bonuses, called Adjusted Compensation certificates, but payment was not scheduled until 1945. The Bonus Army, made up of 12,000 to 15,000 vets, wanted bonuses immediately for help during the Depression. They camped in tents and shacks along the Anacostia River to wait. But when Congress defeated a bill to speed up the bonuses, near-riots ensued, and Army troops forced the vets off the land with tear gas. One vet was shot and killed in the fighting.

10. Answer: B. Erskine Caldwell. Novelist William Faulkner considered Caldwell among the five best contemporary American writers. He was best known for his 1932 novel *Tobacco Road* and 1933's *God's Little Acre*. He also collaborated with his wife-to-be, photographer Margaret Bourke-White, on a powerful documentary book about the Depression-era rural South entitled *You Have Seen Their Faces*.

Questions

★ ★ ★ ★ ★ ★ ★

11. The wages of California laborers fell in the early 1930s as unemployed migrants streamed into the state. By 1938, they were arriving at a rate of 10,000 a month. What were these migrant workers fleeing?

A. Dust storms
B. Earthquake
C. Creditors
D. Legal problems

12. In the mid 1920s, a magazine called *New Masses* was launched. During the Depression, the organization that sponsored *New Masses* enjoyed wider support than at any other period in U.S. history. What was this organization?

A. The Ku Klux Klan
B. The United Auto Workers
C. The American Communist party
D. The Catholic Church

13. In a 1936 article in *Harper's Magazine,* Marquis Childs found wealthy Americans focused much of their hatred on one particular pair of people. Who was the target of so much emotion?

A. Huey Long and Father Coughlin
B. Adolf Hitler and Benito Mussolini
C. Franklin and Eleanor Roosevelt
D. John Dillinger and Al Capone

Answers

★ ★ ★ ★ ★ ★

11. **Answer: A. Dust storms.** A drought in Colorado, Oklahoma, Kansas, New Mexico, and Texas caused dust storms and created what became known as the Dust Bowl. The most dramatic dust storm occurred on May 12, 1934, and carried dust across the East Coast and even out to sea. As the topsoil in these states literally dried up and blew away, unemployed farm workers flooded California. Minimum wage laws were ignored, and contractors took huge cuts of their workers' pay which averaged, in 1935, $289 a year per family.

12. **Answer: C. The American Communist party.** During the '30s, the American Communist party recruited with the slogan: "Communism is 20th Century Americanism." *New Masses,* the party magazine, had a subscription drive with the slogan "I like America."

13. **Answer: C. Franklin and Eleanor Roosevelt.** In the *Harper's* article, "They Hate Roosevelt," Marquis Childs found that the "whole upper stratum of American society" reserved its most abusive language for the people who brought the New Deal to the nation.

QUESTIONS

★ ★ ★ ★ ★ ★ ★

14. In the 1930s people joked that there was only one industry still hiring. What was it?

A. Breadline management
B. Miniature golf
C. The auto industry
D. Government

15. Immediately after the stock market collapse of October 1929, the prestigious *Harvard Economic Society Weekly Letter* predicted a severe depression was outside the range of probability. It continued to print optimistic forecasts until 1931. What changed in that year?

A. The *Weekly Letter* was purchased by *The Wall Street Journal*.
B. The paper was critical of the New Deal.
C. The president urged them to stop.
D. The Harvard Economic Society ran out of funds to publish its newsletter.

16. In a 1974 interview, FDR's aide Rexford Tugwell acknowledged that most of FDR's New Deal programs grew out of ideas from someone outside the administration officials. Who was this person?

A. Eleanor Roosevelt
B. Winston Churchill
C. Herbert Hoover
D. John Maynard Keynes

Answers

14. **Answer: B. Miniature golf.** During these lean years miniature golf, which was inexpensive to play, became a huge fad. The industry employed 200,000 workers and generated profits of more than $225 million in its biggest year. It helped to support the cotton and steel industries as well, because cotton seed hulls were used to surface greens and steel was used in construction of obstacles for trick shots.

15. **Answer: D. The Harvard Economic Society ran out of funds to publish its newsletter.** In its issue for November 15, 1930, the *Weekly Letter* predicted the outlook was for "the end of the decline in business during the early part of 1931 and steady...revival for the remainder of the year." They continued to expect the economy to turn the corner, but their money ran out before it did.

16. **Answer: C. Herbert Hoover.** Despite the fact that history has remembered Hoover as the president who was powerless in the face of the Depression and Franklin Roosevelt as the president who got the nation out, Rexford Tugwell said, "We didn't admit it at the time, but practically the whole New Deal was extrapolated from programs that Hoover started."

QUESTIONS

★ ★ ★ ★ ★ ★ ★

17. From 1935 to 1943, one group produced more than 276 books, 701 pamphlets, and 340 articles and other writings. What group was it?

A. International Workers of the World
B. The Salvation Army
C. Screenwriter's Guild of America
D. Federal Writer's Project

18. This song that was originally written for the 1932 Broadway play *Americana* became an unofficial theme song of the Great Depression. What is the name of the song?

A. "Happy Days Are Here Again"
B. "Brother, Can You Spare a Dime?"
C. "I've Been Working on the Railroad"
D. "This Land Is Your Land"

19. According to a letter written by President Roosevelt in 1933, where did the expression *New Deal* come from?

A. Abraham Lincoln
B. Mark Twain
C. Eleanor Roosevelt
D. Herbert Hoover

Answers

★ ★ ★ ★ ★ ★

17. **Answer: D. Federal Writer's Project.** The Federal Writer's Project (FWP) was part of the New Deal's Works Progress Administration. It employed between 3,500 and 6,700 writers, editors, and researchers. The most well-known material from the FWP was the American Guide Series—a collection of travel guides for each state.

18. **Answer: B. "Brother, Can You Spare a Dime?"** E. Y. "Yip" Harburg wrote the words and Jay Gorney the music to the song that most captured the spirit of the Depression. Harburg was also responsible for the lyrics to some of the songs from the film *The Wizard of Oz*. He penned the lyrics to "Ding-Dong! The Witch Is Dead," "We're Off to See the Wizard," and "Over the Rainbow."

19. **Answer: B. Mark Twain.** On December 8, 1933, FDR wrote to the International Mark Twain Society and said that the name came from the book *A Connecticut Yankee in King Arthur's Court*. In the book, the Yankee says that, in a country where only six people out of a thousand have any voice in the government, the other 994 need a "new deal." Roosevelt apparently thought the phrase was appropriate for the difficult times the country was facing.

QUESTIONS

★ ★ ★ ★ ★ ★ ★ ★

20. The United Auto Worker's union (UAW) was organized in 1935, but General Motors refused to recognize the organization. When they heard rumors that GM was going to move work to factories where the union was weaker, how did the workers in the Flint, Michigan, plant respond?

A. They picketed.
B. They rioted.
C. They held a sit-down strike.
D. They marched on the state capitol.

21. More than 600 banks failed each year between 1921 and 1929, but because they were mostly small, rural banks, the government did not make a move to pass bank insurance legislation. On December 11, 1930, however, another bank closed and made the issue a greater priority. What was the important bank that went under?

A. Bank of America
B. Bank of the United States
C. National Bank of New York
D. New York City Bank

22. In the fall of 1930, more than 6,000 people were peddling a particular product on the corners of New York City that went on to become a memorable symbol of the Depression. What did they sell?

A. Pretzels
B. Apples
C. Oranges
D. Bread

Answers

★ ★ ★ ★ ★ ★

20. **Answer: C. They held a sit-down strike.** Instead of leaving the factory and picketing, which would have allowed GM to bring in other workers, the union members stayed in their normal workplaces and sat. Meanwhile, the union's Women's Auxiliary picketed outside. They also organized a first-aid station, provided child care, and collected food and money for strikers and their families. On March 12, 1937, General Motors agreed to recognize the UAW, and the strike ended. Following this victory, union activity grew throughout the country.

21. **Answer: B. Bank of the United States.** When the Bank of the United States closed in December 1930, it wiped out the savings of nearly half a million people. Another 2,300 banks went out of business in 1931 with no insurance to protect their customers.

22. **Answer: B. Apples.** That year the International Apple Shippers Association discovered it had a surplus of unsold fruit, so it offered the apples on credit to those who were out of work. The apple peddlers sold them on corners for five cents each.

Pop Culture

★ ★ ★ ★ ★ ★ ★ ★ ★ ★ ★

From movies and music to cartoons and comic books, pop culture symbolizes America's lifestyles and leisure activities. The fads and fun that influenced the popular culture of America take us back to the first time we experienced them. Nostalgia lives—all we need do is remember.

1. This Irving Berlin song began life as a rejected number for a 1918 traveling review, *Yip! Yip! Yaphank*. Berlin didn't brush it off again until 1938, when he offered it to Kate Smith to use on her radio show. It became her most famous song and an American favorite. What was its name?

A. "Rose O'Day"
B. "Don't Fence Me In"
C. "God Bless America"
D. "Seems Like Old Times"

2. During the 1930s, spinach consumption increased by 33 percent, an increase that growers attributed directly to what fictional character?

A. The Shadow
B. Rosie the Riveter
C. Uncle Sam
D. Popeye

3. Comedy teams were always popular in the movies, and we seldom think about one member of the team without thinking of the other. True or False: Lou Costello never made a movie without Bud Abbott?

ANSWERS

★ ★ ★ ★ ★ ★ ★

1. **Answer: C. "God Bless America."** Irving Berlin donated all royalties from "God Bless America" to the Boy Scouts and Girl Scouts of America, who have made more than $6 million from it. At various times, some people have wanted to replace "The Star-Spangled Banner" as the national anthem with "God Bless America." But Berlin himself had this to say about the idea: "There's only one national anthem, which can never be replaced."

2. **Answer: D. Popeye.** The spinach-munching character made his comic-strip debut on January 17, 1929, in a strip called "Thimble Theatre." Popeye the Sailor Man wasn't the star of the show, as the comic then focused on Olive Oyl and her family, but he wouldn't stay in the background for long, and soon the stories revolved around him. He became a movie star in 1933. His big screen debut was in a "Betty Boop" cartoon called "Popeye the Sailor" from Fleischer Studios. Nearly 600 Popeye cartoons were to follow.

3. **Answer: False.** Lou Costello appeared solo in the 1959 comedy *The 30-Foot Bride of Candy Rock*. In the film, Costello plays a delivery boy who invents a machine that turns his girlfriend into a giant.

QUESTIONS

★ ★ ★ ★ ★ ★ ★

4. In the 1930s and '40s, a new type of entertainment was becoming popular, but many people didn't like it. New York City Mayor Fiorello La Guardia, in fact, tried to put an end to this fad, which he called "an evil menace to young persons because it develops the gambling urge in children." What was it?

A. Miniature golf
B. Hopscotch
C. Pinball
D. Playing cards

5. Harry Dacre's 1892 song "Daisy Bell" was the most famous song to refer to a craze of the Gay Nineties. What was the craze?

A. Bicycling
B. Wearing bloomers
C. Collecting calling cards
D. Dog shows

6. What do the state of Louisiana, the Illinois Central Railroad, and Arlo Guthrie have in common?

A. The pelican
B. Jazz
C. Gumbo
D. The city of New Orleans

7. In the early 1920s, an Asian game played with tiles made from the shinbones of calves became so popular that manufacturers in China faced a serious shortage of calf shins. They had to order emergency shipments from Chicago slaughterhouses. What was the game?

A. Mah-jongg
B. Dominoes
C. Ouija
D. Canasta

ANSWERS

★ ★ ★ ★ ★ ★

4. **Answer: C. Pinball.** The first real pinball machine was introduced in 1930, but by the end of the decade machines were everywhere. Parents worried about pinball addiction and believed organized crime was behind the craze. In 1942 *The New York Times* reported, "One out of every three persons in the pinball business has been arrested at least once." Fiorello La Guardia banned the game in New York City that year; machines awarding free games are still illegal there, but the law goes unenforced.

5. **Answer: A. Bicycling.** Today "Daisy Bell" is more popularly known as "A Bicycle Built for Two." When automobiles were relatively new at the end of the 19th century, cycling was a huge fad. By 1895, 10 million Americans (out of a total population of about 65 million) owned a bicycle. Other bike songs of the era include "The Cycle Man" and "I Love You, Bicycle and All."

6. **Answer: D. The city of New Orleans.** Louisiana, of course, is home to the city of New Orleans. The Illinois Central Railroad named one of its southbound trains *The City of New Orleans*. Musician Steve Goodman wrote a song about his travels on that train, and the song, "The City of New Orleans," became a 1972 hit for folk singer Arlo Guthrie. (The pelican is the state bird of Louisiana, but it has nothing to do with the Illinois Central Railroad or Guthrie.)

7. **Answer: A. Mah-jongg.** At its height of popularity in 1923, the United States imported more than $1.5 million dollars worth of mah-jongg sets from Shanghai.

Questions

★ ★ ★ ★ ★ ★ ★

8. Drive-in movies created a new way to enjoy the silver screen—you could watch from the comfort of your car. The car also allowed privacy if you wanted to do anything else. How much did the first drive-in movie cost?

A. 10 cents per person
B. 25 cents per person
C. 50 cents per person
D. One dollar per person

9. America's first million-selling song was an 1892 ballad by Charles Harris, about a man who saw his sweetheart kiss another man and ended up alone. Years later the narrator learns that she kissed her brother. The tune was later in the musical *Show Boat*. What was its name?

A. "My Bonnie Lies Over the Ocean"
B. "Jeanie with the Light Brown Hair"
C. "She Wore a Yellow Ribbon"
D. "After the Ball"

10. Walt Disney's TV version of this "king of the wild frontier" kicked off a coonskin cap fad among children of the early 1950s. Who was he?

A. The Lone Ranger
B. Davy Crockett
C. Jesse James
D. Butch Cassidy

11. What children's TV show host worked with puppets named Henrietta Pussycat and King Friday XIII?

A. Fred Rogers
B. Buffalo Bob Smith
C. Captain Kangaroo
D. Shari Lewis

Answers

★ ★ ★ ★ ★ ★

8. **Answer: B. 25 cents per person.** Having received a U.S. patent for his design a month earlier, Richard Hollingshead, Jr., opened the Camden Drive-In Theater in June 1933. The New Jersey-based theater showed *Wife Beware*, starring Adolphe Menjou, entertaining more than 600 carloads of viewers. Hollingshead's design would eventually lead to more than 3,000 "passion pits" (as the outdoor theaters were sometimes called) at their peak in the late 1950s.

9. **Answer: D. "After the Ball."** Before the technology for recording and playing back music was widely available, people used to buy sheet music for their favorite songs to play on the piano and sing. "After the Ball" sold $25,000 a week in sheet music (and that's in 1890s dollars).

10. **Answer: B. Davy Crockett.** Television's Davy, Davy Crockett bore little resemblance to the actual historical figure, but no matter. Kids snapped up lunch boxes, puzzles, and coonskin caps and made Bill Hayes's recording of "The Ballad of Davy Crockett" number one on the charts.

11. **Answer: A. Fred Rogers.** Mister Rogers is best remembered for his sweaters and his line "Won't you be my neighbor?" He created more than 900 half-hour episodes of *Mister Rogers' Neighborhood* before his last show in 2001. The soft-spoken man from Pittsburgh is a Presbyterian minister.

QUESTIONS

★ ★ ★ ★ ★ ★ ★ ★

12. Movies have always captured the imagination. We can see things in movies that can't occur in real life—but they sure look real. One of the most memorable scenes of unreality took place in a 1933 film as the title character climbed to the top of the Empire State Building. What was the movie's name?

A. *Spider-Man*
B. *Rambo*
C. *The Fly*
D. *King Kong*

13. This Canadian-born bandleader was said to play the "Sweetest Music This Side of Heaven." His was the only dance band ever to sell more than 100 million records in the United States. What was his name?

A. Glenn Miller
B. Tommy Dorsey
C. Guy Lombardo
D. Lawrence Welk

14. Actors and actresses start at the bottom and work their way up. Movie and TV stars often appear in small, unnoticeable parts before they are established. What 1980s prime-time soap diva was Anne Bancroft's body double in the poster for the 1967 film *The Graduate*?

A. Joan Collins
B. Michelle Lee
C. Linda Evans
D. Linda Gray

15. Jim Henson, creator of the Muppets, was in the Billboard charts twice: once as the Muppet Ernie singing "Rubber Duckie" and once as Kermit the Frog singing "Rainbow Connection." Which was the bigger hit?

Answers

★ ★ ★ ★ ★ ★ ★

12. Answer: D. *King Kong*. In *King Kong*, the giant gorilla kidnapped Fay Wray and climbed to the top of New York's newest skyscraper. The building itself had only opened in the spring of 1931, so this may have been the first opportunity some moviegoers had to see the building at all.

13. Answer: C. Guy Lombardo. Guy Lombardo and His Royal Canadians charted more than 140 hits from 1927 to 1940, including 21 chart toppers. He is most remembered for his annual New Year's Eve broadcasts, which always ended with his theme song, "Auld Lang Syne." Lombardo died in 1977.

14. Answer: D. Linda Gray. Remember the famous promotional picture with Dustin Hoffman standing in the background, framed by Mrs. Robinson's stockinged leg? That shapely appendage really belonged to the then-unknown model Linda Gray, who later went on to become the long-suffering wife of J. R. Ewing on the TV show *Dallas*. In 2001 Gray took center stage as the cradle-robbing Mrs. Robinson in the London stage production of the story.

15. Answer: "Rubber Duckie." "Rainbow Connection" peaked at number 25 on the charts, while "Rubber Duckie" made it all the way up to number 16.

QUESTIONS

★ ★ ★ ★ ★ ★ ★

16. In 1965 a television situation comedy involving reincarnation debuted. Jerry Van Dyke was the star. What was the name of this TV show?

A. *My Favorite Martian*
B. *My Mother the Car*
C. *My Son Jeep*
D. *My True Story*

17. On August 6, 1956, one of the nation's television networks aired its last telecast of *Boxing from St. Nicholas Arena*. What else was notable about the broadcast?

A. It was the last broadcast of the DuMont network.
B. It was the last time dogfighting was shown on television.
C. It featured a future president named Gerald Ford.
D. It was the first sports event taped in advance for rebroadcast.

18. In the 1930s, a shy, skinny, Ohio high school student named Jerry Siegel wrote a story about a man from another planet who was unassuming by day but secretly had amazing powers. His friend Joe Shuster illustrated it. The pair had no luck selling the idea for several years, but the character would ultimately appear in thousands of comic books, more than 250 newspapers, 13 years of radio shows, several TV series, two movie serials, and a handful of full-length movies. Who was he?

A. Superman
B. Tarzan
C. Captain America
D. Flash Gordon

Answers

★ ★ ★ ★ ★ ★ ★

16. **Answer: B. *My Mother the Car.*** *My Favorite Martian, My Son Jeep,* and *My True Stories* were all actual television shows, but only *My Mother the Car* featured literal re-in-car-nation. Jerry Van Dyke was Dave Crabtree, a bereaved son who discovered his mother had been brought back as a 1928 Porter automobile. The action centered around Crabtree's family, who wanted to trade Mom in for a station wagon, and an evil antique automobile collector desperate to add Mom to his collection. Some critics have called this the worst television show of all time.

17. **Answer: A. It was the last broadcast of the DuMont network.** DuMont was the nation's first televison network and the home of Jackie Gleason and Bishop Fulton J. Sheen. It broadcast the famous Army-McCarthy hearings in their entirety in 1954. But by 1956 only five stations were left to carry the last program feed of this once great network.

18. **Answer: A. Superman.** DC Comics bought all rights to Superman in 1938 for $130. When Jerry Siegel and Joe Shuster tried to get their rights back, DC fired them. The pair kept fighting DC Comics until the late 1970s when Warner Communications, then the owner of DC, finally agreed to pay them $20,000 a year for life. Shuster died in 1992, and Siegel followed in 1996.

QUESTIONS

★ ★ ★ ★ ★ ★ ★

19. A new phrase first appeared in the armed forces newspaper *Yank* on April 30, 1943. Betty Grable was the most famous example of the concept. What was it?

A. Sex symbol
B. It girl
C. Gibson girl
D. Pin-up girl

20. The February 9, 1964, episode of *The Ed Sullivan Show* introduced most Americans to the phenomenon which was the Beatles. It also featured actors from the Broadway production of the musical *Oliver*. The actor playing the Artful Dodger would go on to be cast in the faux-Beatles TV series *The Monkees*. What was his name?

A. Davy Jones
B. Micky Dolenz
C. Mike Nesmith
D. Peter Tork

21. Broadcast on October 30, 1938, an episode of Orson Welles's *Mercury Theater of the Air* was called "radio's moral equivalent to yelling 'fire!' in a crowded theater." By what name is this program commonly known?

A. *Inner Sanctum*
B. *War of the Worlds*
C. *The Shadow*
D. *Gangbusters*

22. The 1952 film *Bwana Devil* featured a new effect that made man-eating lions and missiles seem to leap from the screen. What was this new gimmick called?

A. Technicolor
B. Surround-Sound
C. 3-D
D. Cinemascope

Answers

★ ★ ★ ★ ★ ★

19. **Answer: D. Pin-up girl.** Soldiers during World War II, lacking real-life feminine company, plastered pictures of Betty Grable, Rita Hayworth, and other Hollywood beauties inside their lockers.

20. **Answer: A. Davy Jones.** Then billed as David Jones, the future Monkee sang "I'd Do Anything" between the show-opening and closing appearances of the Fab Four.

21. **Answer: B. *War of the Worlds*.** Listeners who missed the explanatory introduction of *The Mercury Theater of the Air's* adaptation of H. G. Wells's *War of the Worlds* took the drama's "news flashes" as reality and panicked. Radio historians say so many people tuned in to the program late because they had been listening to the popular *Chase & Sanborn Hour* starring Edgar Bergen and Charlie McCarthy and started channel hopping when an unfamiliar singer was introduced. The resulting hysteria from people who honestly thought Earth was being invaded by Martians made the front page of *The New York Times* the next morning.

22. **Answer: C. 3-D.** "Deepies," as they were sometimes called, like *The Creature from the Black Lagoon* and *House of Wax in 3-D*, were the film industry's response to a box-office slump created by television.

THE CIVIL WAR ERA

It was a period of American history that pitted "brother against brother." The Union Army stood toe-to-toe against the Confederate rebels, each fighting to the death for their cause. These people, places, names, and faces from Yankee territory and across the Mason-Dixon Line to the Deep South are among the most well known in all of American history. What's your Civil War I.Q.?

1. One of the most intriguing—and tragic—aspects of the American Civil War is the fact that many Confederate leaders had been prominent in American life before the South seceded from the Union. For instance, military leaders from both sides of the Civil War had previously been soldiers together in the same army. In what war did Robert E. Lee and Ulysses S. Grant serve together?

A. Mexican-American War
B. Black Hawk War
C. Mormon War
D. Spanish-American War

2. South Carolina was the first state to secede from the Union, in December 1860, and ten other states ultimately followed. Which one of the following states did *not* secede from the Union during the Civil War?

A. Texas
B. Louisiana
C. Kentucky
D. Florida

Answers

★ ★ ★ ★ ★ ★ ★

1. Answer: A. Mexican-American War. The war between the United States and its southern neighbor (1846–1848) was a proving ground for military greats from both the Union and the Confederacy, including Thomas Jackson (who later earned the nickname "Stonewall" at Bull Run), P.G.T. Beauregard, and Joseph Hooker. In fact, when Robert E. Lee surrendered to Ulysses S. Grant at Appomattox Court House, the two shared reminiscences of their previous meeting during that war. Although the Americans were often greatly outnumbered during the Mexican conflict, they repeatedly defeated Mexican forces. In the treaty that ended the war, Mexico ceded more than 500,000 square miles of territory to the United States, including land that would become California, New Mexico, Arizona, and Utah.

2. Answer: C. Kentucky. Kentucky initially declared itself a neutral state in the war—the governor wanted to secede, while the legislature was staunchly Unionist. In September 1861, however, the border state aligned itself with the North. Kentucky was one of four states (along with Maryland, Delaware, and Missouri) that did not join the Confederacy even though citizens in those states could legally own slaves.

QUESTIONS

★ ★ ★ ★ ★ ★ ★

3. Before the Civil War, the issue of slavery drew high emotions in all parts of the country and was the focus of much public debate. What renowned slave filed suit in 1846 to gain his or her freedom in a case that ultimately went all the way to the Supreme Court?

A. Dred Scott
B. Frederick Douglass
C. Harriet Tubman
D. Nat Turner

4. In another example of Confederate leaders coming from the top ranks of U.S. officials, Confederate President Jefferson Davis had been a senator from Mississippi and secretary of war under President Franklin Pierce. He was also a graduate of which one of these military institutions?

A. Virginia Military Institute
B. The Citadel
C. U.S. Military Academy at West Point
D. National War College

5. The secession of the Southern states caused a lot of social and political upheaval throughout the country. Alliances shifted, old institutions faded away, and new institutions took their place. One obvious result of this was the creation of new states. Which of these U.S. states was formed as a direct result of the Confederacy's secession from the Union?

A. North Dakota
B. Kansas
C. West Virginia
D. Wisconsin

Answers

★ ★ ★ ★ ★ ★

3. **Answer: A. Dred Scott.** The Supreme Court's 1857 Dred Scott decision ruled that Scott, as a slave and a black man, was not a U.S. citizen and therefore could not sue his owner, John Sandford. In the 7–2 decision, the Southern-controlled court also declared that the Missouri Compromise of 1820 was unconstitutional and the federal government had no power to prohibit slavery in the territories. The Dred Scott case was a severe blow to abolitionists, and it inflamed sectional tensions between the North and the South.

4. **Answer: C. U.S. Military Academy at West Point.** Jefferson Davis spent four years at West Point and graduated in 1828 as a second lieutenant. He later served as an officer in the Black Hawk War and the Mexican War. The New York military institution graduated more Civil War officers—both Union and Confederate—than any other school.

5. **Answer: C. West Virginia.** This region was part of Virginia when that state left the Union in 1861. But many in the western counties were already unhappy with their leaders in Richmond and took the opportunity to break and run. West Virginia gained admittance to the United States on April 20, 1863.

QUESTIONS

★ ★ ★ ★ ★ ★ ★

6. In 1862, America's first clash of ironclad warships occurred between the *Monitor* and the *Merrimack* off the coast of Virginia. True or False: In the battle, the *Monitor* defeated the *Merrimack*.

7. Many people know that Confederate soldiers were called Johnny Rebs, but what term was used to describe members of the Union Army?

A. Billy Yanks
B. Union Joes
C. Jimmy Norths
D. Lincoln's Lads

8. Approximately how many people died on both sides of the Civil War?

A. 330,000
B. 450,000
C. 620,000
D. 1,100,000

9. During the Civil War, a lot of property and land was confiscated for military purposes. True or False: Arlington Cemetery was once the site of Robert E. Lee's home.

Answers

★ ★ ★ ★ ★ ★ ★

6. Answer: False. While the Union Army's *Monitor* was equipped with a revolving turret that held two large guns, it fought to a draw with the Confederate ship *Merrimack*, which was originally a wooden steamship that had been sunk in 1861. The Confederates raised the ship, fitted it with protective metal plates, and renamed it the *Virginia*. Both ships sank before the end of the war, with parts of the *Merrimack* being recovered in 1875. A major effort to recover the *Monitor* continued into 2001, with crews raising the 30-ton steam engine and propeller.

7. Answer: A. Billy Yanks. The name, along with Johnny Rebs, is the equivalent of World War II's G.I. Joes.

8. Answer: C. 620,000. The Union saw roughly 360,000 troops die in battle or from disease, while the Confederacy suffered 260,000 deaths. Add another 375,000 wounded, and casualties totaled more than three percent of the country's population at the war's start. By comparison, about 400,000 Americans died in World War II.

9. Answer: True. Arlington was originally owned by George Washington Parke Custis, who intended it to be a living memorial to his adopted grandfather, George Washington. After Custis's death in 1857, the property passed to his daughter, who had married Robert E. Lee in 1831. Early in the war, Lee and his wife abandoned the estate, which later became a Union Army headquarters. During the war, 200 acres were set aside for a cemetery for Union troops. Freedman's Village, a model community for freed slaves, was also established on this site.

QUESTIONS

★ ★ ★ ★ ★ ★ ★

10. A great deal of heroism was present in both the North and the South during the Civil War. What officer yelled to his men, "Damn the torpedoes! Full speed ahead"?

A. Charles Wilkes
B. Samuel du Pont
C. Franklin Buchanan
D. David G. Farragut

11. The Confederacy had a number of able leaders, but one received special attention in the Northern states. Who was known in the North as "the Brains of the Confederacy"?

A. Judah P. Benjamin
B. Nathan Bedford Forrest
C. George E. Pickett
D. Thomas "Stonewall" Jackson

12. What was the name of the Civil War's most infamous prisoner-of-war camp?

A. Chancellorsville
B. Fort Sill
C. Andersonville
D. Stringtown

ANSWERS

★ ★ ★ ★ ★ ★

10. **Answer: D. David G. Farragut.** Admiral Farragut commanded the Union fleet that captured New Orleans in 1862 and was given the responsibility of blockading the Gulf Coast. A lot of cargo was being smuggled through the blockade from Mobile, Alabama, and Farragut became impatient. Although Mobile Bay was heavily defended and scattered with Confederate torpedoes (unlike modern torpedoes, these were stationary mines that exploded on contact), Farragut decided to take it by force. At one point in the battle the Union ironclad *Tecumseh* struck a torpedo and sank. When the other captains hesitated, Farragut shouted out his now-famous line.

11. **Answer: A. Judah P. Benjamin.** Benjamin was a close advisor to Jefferson Davis and served in his cabinet as secretary of war (1861–1862) and then state (1862–1865). But before the South seceded, he was the first openly professing Jewish member of the U.S. Senate, where he staunchly defended the legal basis for slavery. After the war, Benjamin escaped the Union Army and fled to England, where he continued to practice law.

12. **Answer: C. Andersonville.** The Andersonville stockade in the heart of Georgia was built to house fewer than 10,000 Union prisoners, but by August 1864, more than 33,000 POWs were crammed in there under terrible conditions. Nearly 13,000 soldiers died of disease, poor sanitation, malnutrition, overcrowding, or exposure to the elements. Andersonville was one of many POW camps, but its commander, Captain Henry Wirz, was the only soldier to be executed for his actions during the war.

Questions

★ ★ ★ ★ ★ ★ ★

13. The exploits of one Civil War hero led to his appointment as the youngest general in American history. Who was he?

A. Ambrose Everett Burnside
B. George Armstrong Custer
C. Braxton Bragg
D. John C. Fremont

14. Much of the fighting during the Civil War was limited to Southern land, but Confederate forces made some successful excursions north. What was the northernmost U.S. city to be attacked by Confederate forces?

A. Saratoga, New York
B. Manchester, New Hampshire
C. Worcester, Massachusetts
D. St. Albans, Vermont

15. True or False: President Abraham Lincoln scribbled the Gettysburg address on the back of an envelope as he was traveling to the battleground by train.

Answers

★ ★ ★ ★ ★ ★ ★

13. **Answer: B. George Armstrong Custer.** Even though Custer graduated under a disciplinary cloud at the bottom of his class at West Point, his flair and brave recklessness propelled him to the rank of brigadier general. Incidentally, it was because of Union General Ambrose Burnside's trademark muttonchops that the word "sideburn" entered the English language.

14. **Answer: D. St. Albans, Vermont.** In early October 1864, several men checked into a hotel in sleepy St. Albans, 15 miles south of the Canadian border. On each of the next few days, two or three more men disguised as tourists arrived until there were about 20 in total. They were a friendly group, at least until October 19, when the group simultaneously robbed three area banks. The plan was executed with the full knowledge of the Confederacy, and the money was intended to go into rebel coffers. The raiders escaped over the border only to be captured by Canadian police.

15. **Answer: False.** The train part is true, as Abraham Lincoln was still finalizing his words on the morning of his speech, but the rest is just a myth. Lincoln always prepared his speeches very carefully, and he knew the important opportunity that this one provided. A number of drafts of the speech have surfaced over the years, including one on executive stationery written in his own hand. His 272-word address, short and to the point, stood in stark contrast to the two-hour speech given by the day's other orator, former Massachusetts governor Edward Everett.

QUESTIONS

★ ★ ★ ★ ★ ★ ★

16. Washington, D.C., on the Potomac River between Maryland and Virginia, is a fair distance south of the Mason-Dixon Line. Virginia and the Confederacy lay just across the river. During the Civil War, the capital of the United States was always a potential target. True or False: In 1864, Confederate troops came within 30 miles of mounting an attack on Washington.

17. The "War Between the States" raged on for four long years, from 1861 to 1865. Once it was all over, how much had the war cost both sides, in dollars?

A. $8.3 billion
B. $6.6 million
C. $1.4 billion
D. $77 million

18. Much has been written about the Lincoln assassination. True or False: John Wilkes Booth acted alone when he assassinated President Abraham Lincoln.

ANSWERS

★★★★★★

16. **Answer: True.** Confederate General Robert E. Lee, desperate to offset attacks by Union generals Ulysses S. Grant and William Tecumseh Sherman on Southern cities, sent General Jubal Early to strike the United States capital. Even though he had the Capitol dome in his view, the Confederate general was turned away by Union troops, led by General Lew Wallace. It may have been a case of Early being too late.

17. **Answer: A. $8.3 billion.** In 1879, the government estimated that Union Army costs totaled nearly $6.2 billion. For its part, the Confederacy spent more than $2.1 billion. What's more, by 1906, another $3.3 billion was spent by the U.S. government on pensions and other veterans' benefits for former Union soldiers. Southern states and private philanthropy provided benefits to Confederate veterans.

18. **Answer: False.** John Wilkes Booth was the ringleader of a larger conspiracy hatched in a Washington boardinghouse and meant to take the lives of other government leaders as well. A second conspirator, former Confederate soldier Lewis Paine (whose real name was Louis Thornton Powell), went to Secretary of State William H. Seward's house and managed to stab him before escaping. The group also planned attacks against General Ulysses S. Grant and Vice-President Andrew Johnson but never attempted to carry them out. Most of Booth's conspirators were captured after he was killed in a shootout on April 26, 1865, and four of them were hanged.

SCIENCE AND TECHNOLOGY

America has always been a nation of innovations and inventors. Advancements in science and technology helped shape the history of the United States. Whether they were advances in transportation, communications, architecture, medicine, chemistry, digital technology, or many other fields, Americans were often there to lead the way. Now you take the lead to find out what you know—after all, it's not "rocket science"... or, is it?

1. Thomas Alva Edison may be the most influential inventor America has ever seen. Known as the "Wizard of Menlo Park," Edison patented 1,093 inventions, including the incandescent light bulb and the phonograph. Edison's laboratories were also instrumental in devising the motion picture camera and viewer—the first motion picture to be copyrighted was created in the Edison labs. What action did this film portray?

A. Women dancing
B. A man sneezing
C. A tennis match
D. A bank robbery

2. In 1951 the U.S. Census installed UNIVAC (Universal Automatic Computer), the first computer to be used for commercial purposes. Just for curiosity's sake, how much memory did UNIVAC have?

A. 1.5 kilobytes (K)
B. 10 kilobytes (K)
C. 64 kilobytes (K)
D. 40 megabytes (MB)

ANSWERS

★ ★ ★ ★ ★ ★

1. Answer: B. A man sneezing. The 1894 *Edison Kinetoscopic Record of a Sneeze* was 47 frames long and featured Fred Ott, an Edison employee known by his coworkers for his comic sneezes and other gags. The motion picture technology was so new that this motion picture was submitted to the Copyright Office as a series of 47 sequential photographs rather than as a celluloid film.

2. Answer: A. 1.5 kilobytes (K). In the 1950s UNIVAC was considered a true miracle of science, an example of the high-tech future that undoubtedly was to come. It cost between $1 and $1.5 million, the equivalent of $6.5 million to $9.8 million today. But even with this scientific marvel, people who should have known better still didn't realize what they had on their hands. In 1977 Ken Olson, the president of computer-maker Digital Equipment Corporation, said, "There is no reason for any individual to have a computer in their home." And as late as 1981, Microsoft's Bill Gates made the claim, "640K ought to be enough for anybody." Fifty years after UNIVAC, consumers can purchase a typical home computer with memory of 128 megabytes and more, 85,000 times what UNIVAC had. If that home computer comes with a processing chip of one gigahertz, it can add numbers 26,000 times faster than UNIVAC ever did.

QUESTIONS

★ ★ ★ ★ ★ ★ ★

3. In 1852 Elisha Graves Otis rode to a considerable height in an elevator then had the cable cut while he was still inside. Why would Otis perform such a dangerous act?

A. To test an invention
B. To win a bet
C. To measure the elevator's speed as it fell
D. To raise his heart rate

4. True or False: In the early days of the automobile, environmentalists protested against the pollution the new device caused.

5. Once it became available, recorded music, first on cylinders, then on discs and 78-rpm records, was very popular with American consumers. But in 1948 that popularity exploded when a new medium for recorded music was introduced. A 15-inch stack of these new items could play as much music as an 8-foot tower of the old 78s. What was the new medium?

A. LPs
B. Compact Discs
C. 8-track tapes
D. Reel-to-reel tapes

6. True or False: The invention of the silk hat caused many small lakes and bogs to appear throughout the United States.

Answers

★ ★ ★ ★ ★ ★ ★

3. Answer: A. To test an invention. Elisha Graves Otis devised the first elevator to include a built-in safety device that would lower the elevator car slowly if anything happened to the cord. He successfully tested it himself.

4. Answer: False. Cars were seen as a solution to the problem of pollution. Prior to the automobile, horses created a different kind of pollution. At the beginning of the last century in New York City, horses left 2.5 million pounds of manure and 60,000 gallons of urine on the streets each day.

5. Answer: A. LPs. The 33⅓-rpm long-playing record or LP eventually made the hundreds of millions of 78s produced up to that time obsolete. Although 8-track and cassette tapes would eat into its popularity, the LP reigned supreme until the 1980s, when compact discs forced it aside as the LP had previously done to the 78s.

6. Answer: True. As odd as it may sound, there was a direct link between silk hats and a higher number of lakes and bogs. When men started sporting silk hats in the 1830s and '40s, the demand fell for other previously popular types of hats. One hat-making material that had been used extensively was beaver pelt. Beaver trapping dropped off considerably, and the beaver population flourished. More beavers, of course, meant more dams to create more lakes and bogs.

QUESTIONS

★ ★ ★ ★ ★ ★ ★

7. True or False: The first steamboat was invented by Robert Fulton.

8. Blood-plasma pioneer Charles Drew was the first medical director of the American Red Cross Blood Bank in 1941. He resigned in protest soon after. Why?

A. He refused to accept blood from women.
B. He did not want to supply blood for war.
C. He was offended that he was not promoted.
D. He disagreed with a rule categorizing blood by race.

9. In 1848 Charles Burton invented something that caused a stir in his home of New York City. Initially, New Yorkers protested against his invention because pedestrians tended to get hit with it. What did he invent?

A. A motorized bicycle
B. Roller skates
C. A baby carriage
D. A shopping cart

10. The first building known as a "skyscraper" was erected in Chicago by the Home Insurance Company of New York. Construction began on May 1, 1884, and took a little more than a year to complete. How tall was this building?

A. 5 stories
B. 10 stories
C. 50 stories
D. 100 stories

Answers

★ ★ ★ ★ ★ ★

7. Answer: False. The first working steamboat, which could only navigate short trips, was made in 1783 by a Frenchman named Claude de Jouffroy d'Abbans. In 1790 a Connecticut man, John Fitch, tried to operate a commercial steamboat but couldn't make it profitable. He was awarded a U.S. patent for the steamboat in 1791. Robert Fulton's successful modifications on the *Clermont* made boats with steam engines efficient and viable as commercial vessels, ushering in a new era of water travel.

8. Answer: D. He disagreed with a rule categorizing blood by race. An African American, Dr. Charles Drew was offended by a regulation that kept "black blood" separate from blood donated by white people. A misconception surrounds Drew's 1950 death. After a North Carolina automobile accident, Drew was treated at a segregated hospital. Although doctors did their utmost, he died of his injuries. A widely repeated but incorrect myth claims Drew was turned away from this hospital because of race, denied the lifesaving treatment he had pioneered.

9. Answer: C. A baby carriage. Charles Burton left New York for England, where he opened a factory to make "perambulators." His customers included such royalty as England's Queen Victoria and Queen Isabella II of Spain.

10. Answer: B. 10 stories. The Home Insurance building, nine floors and a basement, was made of a steel frame supporting marble walls. Two stories were later added for a grand total of 12. By comparison, Sears Tower in Chicago, which opened in 1973, has 110 stories.

QUESTIONS

★ ★ ★ ★ ★ ★ ★

11. Advances in medical care progressed quickly in the 19th century, and America was often right in the middle of them. In 1865 Commercial Hospital in Cincinnati became the first U.S. hospital to provide what?

A. A full-time surgical staff
B. Surgical masks
C. Ambulance service
D. Pillows

12. Chemist and physicist Glenn Theodore Seaborg of the University of California at Berkeley discovered the 95th and 96th elements, americium and curium, in 1944. Where did Seaborg announce his discovery of these elements to the world?

A. At a meeting of the American Chemical Society
B. In the journal *Science*
C. On a billboard
D. On a children's radio quiz show

13. Samuel F. B. Morse invented the telegraph in 1844, sending a series of electrical dots and dashes along a copper wire strung between Washington, D.C., and Baltimore. His first message asked, "What hath God wrought?" How did Morse finance his communications research?

A. As mayor of New York
B. As a surveyor
C. As a house painter
D. As a portrait painter

Answers

★ ★ ★ ★ ★ ★ ★

11. Answer: C. Ambulance service. James A. Jackson was paid $360 a year as the first recorded ambulance driver. Before this, those needing hospital care had to get there on their own. Bellevue Hospital in New York started a similar service in 1869.

12. Answer: D. On a children's radio quiz show. Shortly after Glenn Theodore Seaborg observed the birth of two new elements in the cyclotron of the University of California at Berkeley's radiation lab, he was invited to be a panelist on the radio show *Quiz Kids*, in which bright children quizzed experts. Although the discovery was scheduled to be announced at a meeting of the American Chemical Society, while on the show he was asked if there were any new elements. He revealed the new discovery in response.

13. Answer: D. As a portrait painter. Samuel F. B. Morse supported his experiments in telegraphy by using his well-developed talents as an artist. Coming from a well-to-do family, Morse was a member of the British Royal Academy of Art and was instrumental in creating the National Academy of Design in New York City. He almost *did* become mayor of New York, though, running twice and losing twice.

Questions

★ ★ ★ ★ ★ ★ ★

14. When Willis H. Carrier built the first effective air-conditioning unit in 1902, his goal was not to cool the room down to make it comfortable for human beings. What was he trying to do?

A. Keep the animals in his veterinary practice cool
B. Keep medications at the proper temperature
C. Prevent coated papers from contracting and expanding
D. Keep his industrial equipment from overheating

15. True or False: Designer John A. Roebling received the key to the city of New York at the opening of his most famous design, the Brooklyn Bridge.

16. Although medical knowledge wasn't great in the 19th century (doctors still prescribed bloodletting at mid-century), medical treatment advanced quickly. One example of this advancement took place on October 16, 1846. On this day, Thomas Morton of Boston's Massachusetts General Hospital first demonstrated the use of something. What was it?

A. Ether as a general anesthetic
B. A smallpox vaccine
C. Surgical gloves
D. A gurney

Answers

★ ★ ★ ★ ★ ★ ★

14. **Answer: C. Prevent coated papers from contracting and expanding.** Willis H. Carrier, an employee of the Buffalo Forge Company, was sent to the Sackett-Wilhelms Lithographing and Publishing Company of Brooklyn to find a way to protect the coated papers used in their work. When the weather got hot and humid, these coated papers would change shape. The first commercial use of air-conditioning to make people more comfortable did not come for another 15 years, when the Central Park Theater of Chicago installed a system.

15. **Answer: False.** John A. Roebling did not live to see the 1883 opening of the Brooklyn Bridge. In 1869, while visiting the bridge site before construction began, he was injured, developed tetanus, and died. His son Washington took over the project, but he had health problems of his own. In 1873 he suffered the bends while working in pressurized concrete chambers under the river. He became so ill and weak that he had to direct construction from his home, but he did manage to see the project through.

16. **Answer: A. Ether as a general anesthetic.** Before ether was used as an anesthetic, doctors had little that could effectively dull a patient's pain during surgery. One historian has said that surgeons sometimes brought two bottles of whiskey into an operation—one for the patient and one for the surgeon, who had to listen to the patient's screams. Patients, who felt almost everything, were tied down for surgery and frequently died of shock.

THE WEST: FRONTIER TRIVIA

★ ★

Mount up the horses and move out the wagon train—it's time for a trip to the Wild, Wild West. Imagine the smell of gun smoke and rawhide, as you look for a bonanza of American courage. Do you have what it takes to test your frontier knowledge?

1. Although the frontier had existed throughout American history, after the Civil War it seemed to open up as a land of unlimited promise. A frequent piece of advice heard in the 19th century was "Go West, young man." Who originally made this suggestion?

A. Brigham Young
B. John Soule
C. Andrew Jackson
D. Horace Greeley

2. Covered wagons rolling west along the trail have become an American icon. These vehicles were sometimes called by another name—what was it?

A. Prairie schooners
B. Land rollers
C. Trailblazers
D. Westland wagons

3. In 1856 John C. Fremont was the first presidential candidate ever put forward by the Republican Party. What was Fremont's contribution to Western expansion?

A. He led the first wagon train across the Mississippi River.
B. He mapped out the Oregon Trail.
C. He climbed to the top of Pikes Peak.
D. He was the first governor of California.

ANSWERS

★ ★ ★ ★ ★ ★ ★

1. Answer: B. John Soule. Although the statement has often been credited to Horace Greeley, it was actually first penned by Soule, a reporter in Indiana, in 1851. Greeley popularized the sentiments as the influential founder and editor of the *New York Tribune*, but he tried to provide Soule with proper credit for the quote. Little else is commonly known about Soule. Greeley was a social reformer and a vocal supporter of the abolitionist, temperance, and women's rights movements. He ran for president against Ulysses S. Grant in 1872.

2. Answer: A. Prairie schooners. So named because their canvas coverings billowed like the sails of sea schooners, the wagons formed "trains" that sometimes stretched for five miles. Covered wagons were also called "Conestogas," after the Pennsylvania town where they were built. During the Gold Rush, one point at the Mississippi River saw 12,000 wagons headed west. But the advent of railroads in the 1870s marked the end of the prairie schooner.

3. Answer: B. He mapped out the Oregon Trail. The 2,000-mile route of the trail stretched from Independence, Missouri, to the Columbia River in Oregon. John C. Fremont made several journeys along the trail, each time more clearly defining the way westward. He eventually became one of the first two senators from California, where the city of Fremont is named for him. His unsuccessful presidential bid was against James Buchanan. Fremont was later appointed governor of the Arizona Territory in 1878.

Questions

★ ★ ★ ★ ★ ★ ★

4. Originally a Franciscan mission in San Antonio, the Alamo was a fort in the Texan fight against Mexico. In February 1836, General Antonio López de Santa Anna led 2,000 Mexican soldiers against the 150 at the Alamo. The siege lasted into March, when the remaining warriors fought hand-to-hand with Mexican troops inside the garrison. All 150 Texans were killed, along with 600 Mexican soldiers. The cry "Remember the Alamo" helped defeat Santa Anna later at the Battle of San Jacinto. Which of these brave Americans did *not* fight at the Alamo?

A. Jim Bowie
B. William Travis
C. Daniel Boone
D. Davy Crockett

5. When European pioneers started to head west, buffalo were plentiful. Estimates of the American buffalo population range from 30 to 75 million. When scouting through today's South Dakota, Lewis and Clark reported seeing a "moving multitude which darkened the whole plains." Although it is commonly called the buffalo, this animal has a more accurate name. What is it?

A. The ox
B. The bison
C. The wood buffalo
D. The wisent

6. In 1881 at the O.K. Corral, the "guys in the white hats," the Earp brothers and Doc Holliday, took on the Clanton Gang. Just what kind of "doc" was Holliday?

A. A general practitioner
B. A dentist
C. A foot doctor
D. A bone specialist

ANSWERS

★ ★ ★ ★ ★ ★

4. Answer: C. Daniel Boone. Boone, born in 1734, died 16 years before the Alamo. He helped blaze the Cumberland Gap trail from Virginia into Kentucky and Tennessee. By the way, Fess Parker played both Boone and Davy Crockett on television during the '50s and '60s.

5. Answer: B. The bison. The bison was a friend to Native Americans of the Great Plains. It provided food, clothing, and bones for tools. Once pioneers started the trek west, the bison began to disappear at an astounding rate. Big-game hunters, Wild West shows, and hide skinners all contributed to the demise of the animal. By the late 1880s, American buffalo numbers dwindled to less than 1,000.

6. Answer: B. A dentist. Originally from Georgia, John Henry Holliday practiced dentistry in the East. But he contracted tuberculosis and, in 1872, headed west for the drier climate. On the frontier he quickly gained a reputation as a gambler and gunfighter. In 1881 U.S. Marshal Virgil Earp deputized his brothers, Wyatt and Morgan, and Holliday, intending to clear the cattle-rustling Clanton Gang out of Tombstone, Arizona. Three Clanton members were killed in the Gunfight at the O.K. Corral, which became a legend in Western lore.

QUESTIONS

★ ★ ★ ★ ★ ★ ★

7. In 1866, as Americans headed West after the Civil War, Congress decided a new coin was needed. What coin was introduced?

A. The penny
B. The nickel
C. The dime
D. The quarter

8. The West seemed to produce individuals who were larger than life, and many of these people are commonly remembered today. Which of these Native Americans was a leader of the Apaches?

A. Geronimo
B. Sitting Bull
C. Crazy Horse
D. Red Cloud

9. One of the most exciting chapters in the history of the American West was the Pony Express mail service. Pony Express carriers raced to bring mail to the West in record time. Before the Pony Express, how long did it take for mail to be delivered cross-country?

A. One week
B. Two weeks
C. Three weeks
D. One month

Answers

★ ★ ★ ★ ★ ★

7. Answer: B. The nickel. Many coins, each a fraction of the dollar, were already in existence, including the half cent, large cent, copper-nickel cent, two-cent piece, three-cent nickel, three-cent silver, and silver half-dime. U.S. Mint Director James Pollack had resisted issuing coins made from nickel, since the hard metal was difficult to strike and could damage the Mint's machines. He finally realized the need for the five-cent nickel, and it was issued, with the U.S. shield on one side and the numeral 5 on the other.

8. Answer: A. Geronimo. A leader of the Chiricahua Apache people, Geronimo received his sobriquet from Mexican soldiers (it is the Spanish version of *Jerome*). His Native American name was Goyathlay or "one who yawns." Sitting Bull was a Hunkpapa Lakota chief, while Crazy Horse and Red Cloud were both leaders of the Oglala Lakota.

9. Answer: C. Three weeks. The Pony Express mail service, which cut delivery time down to eight days, started in 1860. Riders took mail by horseback from St. Joseph, Missouri, to Sacramento, California. Changing stations were spaced at specific intervals, where riders and their cargo could be switched. Young, lightweight riders were equipped with special saddlebags for quick and easy transfer between horses as necessary. The success of the Pony Express was short-lived, however. By 1861, the telegraph lines extended to San Francisco, and the Pony Express was obsolete.

Questions

★ ★ ★ ★ ★ ★ ★

10. The discovery of gold in California created the "Gold Rush," starting in 1849. Many of the gold miners became known as "Forty-niners," but they also had another nickname. What was it?

A. The Argonauts
B. The Gringos Oro
C. The Pan Scrapers
D. The Mine Pickers

11. Frontiersman Wild Bill Hickok was killed while playing poker in 1876. The cards he held at that time are known to this day as the "dead man's hand." What poker hand was Hickok holding?

A. Four jacks
B. Three sevens and two kings
C. Two aces and two eights
D. Three tens

12. Not everyone who contributed to taming the Wild West did so behind the barrel of a gun. Joseph Glidden, a very "un-cowpoke" sort of man, created something to make life easier on the frontier. What was it?

A. A refined Western saddle
B. Barbed wire
C. Coaxial telegraph cable
D. Boot spurs

Answers

★ ★ ★ ★ ★ ★ ★

10. **Answer: A. The Argonauts.** The term means "gold traveler." The first California Argonaut might have been James Marshall. As a carpenter, Marshall was building a sawmill for John Sutter in northern California when he discovered gold on the site. Although sworn to secrecy, Sutter's workers spread the word, and soon gold seekers came from as far away as Australia and China. By 1852, more than 200,000 people had found their way to the Sacramento Valley, seeking the riches of gold.

11. **Answer: C. Two aces and two eights.** James Butler Hickok had been a farmer, a constable, a stagecoach driver, and even a Union spy during the Civil War. He was a scout for Lieutenant Colonel George Custer and became U.S. Marshal in several Kansas towns. Wild Bill joined Buffalo Bill's Wild West Show in the early 1870s. Married and mining for gold in 1876, Hickok was fatally shot in the back by a drifter named Jack McCall.

12. **Answer B. Barbed wire.** Joseph Glidden, a farmer in DeKalb, Illinois, patented barbed wire in 1874, realizing that wood was too expensive for cattle ranchers to use for fencing. Some Western ranches were tens of thousands of square miles. In just a few years, Glidden's plant was turning out more than 80 million pounds of barbed wire annually. But the invention had a downside: It caused "fence wars" between farmers, who could now clearly mark their property boundaries, and cattle herders, who had become accustomed to moving their livestock over unrestricted, "straight-line" trails.

Questions

★ ★ ★ ★ ★ ★ ★

13. Jim Bowie, one of the heroes who died at the Alamo, is almost synonymous with a particular weapon. What was this weapon?

A. Rifle
B. Knife
C. Bayonet
D. Bow and arrow

14. Cowboys on the range, driving their cattle on long drives to market, camping around a fire every night, is one of the defining images of Western lore. The most significant drives took place along the rugged and historic Chisholm Trail. What two cities were connected by the Chisholm Trail?

A. San Antonio, Texas, and Abilene, Kansas
B. El Paso, Texas, and Denver, Colorado
C. Amarillo, Texas, and Omaha, Nebraska
D. Waco, Texas, and Little Rock, Arkansas

15. As railroads spread out across the country, an effort quickly began to connect the two coasts by train. What two railroads met to form the first transcontinental railroad in 1869?

A. The Southern Pacific and the Santa Fe
B. The Union Pacific and the Central Pacific
C. The Great Northern and the New York Central
D. The Illinois Central and the Grand Trunk Railway

Answers

★ ★ ★ ★ ★ ★

13. **Answer: B. Knife.** Many people think "Big Jim" invented the bowie knife, but evidence shows that it was actually the design of his brother Rezin. The famed knife, with its 15-inch curved blade, was popularized because of its connection to the legendary Alamo fighter, who is said to have used it to cut down many Mexican soldiers while he lay in his cot stricken with pneumonia.

14. **Answer: A. San Antonio, Texas, and Abilene, Kansas.** Jesse Chisholm, half-Scot and half-Cherokee, mapped out a route in 1867 for cattle breeders to move their livestock north for shipping east. The trip along the trail took about four months, winding its way through Indian Territory and crossing the dangerous Red River. By the mid-1880s, railroads had been put through, and the Chisholm Trail was no longer necessary.

15. **Answer: B. The Union Pacific and the Central Pacific.** The cowcatchers of steam engines from both railroads gently touched at Promontory Summit, Utah, on May 10, 1869. The golden spike on the last piece of train track had been driven by the man who spearheaded the cross-country efforts, Central Pacific President Leland Stanford. (Some accounts indicate that Stanford missed and the ceremonial spike was actually driven by one of the workers standing nearby.)

Questions

★ ★ ★ ★ ★ ★ ★ ★

16. The tales of the Wild West often feature the thrilling stories of lawman Bat Masterson. The famous sheriff eventually tired of gunfights, however, and changed careers. What did Masterson become?

A. A minister
B. A dry goods shop owner
C. A dance hall piano player
D. A newspaper reporter

17. Everything has to come from somewhere, and sometimes an item's point of origin is quite unexpected. True or False: The ten-gallon hat was invented in Philadelphia.

18. Men and women both contributed to taming the Wild West, of course, and one of the most famous women was legendary for her target-shooting ability. In fact, to call her an expert shot would be a huge understatement—she could hit a thrown playing card with a dozen bullets before it landed on the ground. Who was this renowned sharpshooter?

A. Annie Oakley
B. Lola Montez
C. Belle Starr
D. Lillie Langtry

Answers

★ ★ ★ ★ ★ ★ ★

16. **Answer: D. A newspaper reporter.** William Barclay "Bat" Masterson hailed from Illinois, but he was elected sheriff of Ford County, Kansas, in 1877 while still in his twenties. Based out of Dodge City, Masterson traveled to Tombstone, Arizona, where he helped Marshal Wyatt Earp bring law and order to the territory. By 1902, Masterson had moved to New York City, where he became a sportswriter for the *New York Morning Telegraph*. Gaining a reputation as an expert on boxing, Masterson continued to cover sports until he died of natural causes at his desk in 1921.

17. **Answer: True.** John Stetson, a well-known Philadelphia haberdasher, needed something to boost business. A trip to the Midwest reminded him that the cattle barons from the big state of Texas liked everything king-size. Stetson designed the broad-brimmed, tall-crowned ten-gallon Western cowboy hat (which really only has the capacity for about one gallon). The hat became known as "The Boss of the Plains" and was the standard for cowboys for years.

18. **Answer: A. Annie Oakley.** Born in a rustic log cabin, Phoebe Anne Oakley Mosee learned to use a rifle at the age of six to help feed her family. She soon became a professional game hunter and joined Buffalo Bill's Wild West show at the age of 25.

Questions

★ ★ ★ ★ ★ ★ ★ ★

19. In 1876 Lieutenant Colonel George Armstrong Custer led his troops against a Lakota village at Little Bighorn. Wildly overconfident, Custer believed that his 265 soldiers could easily defeat the village. He was wrong. The U.S. soldiers were completely wiped out. How many Native Americans did the regiment come up against?

A. 500
B. 1,200
C. 1,700
D. 2,500

20. The U.S. government tried various tactics against Native Americans in the West, ranging from Congressional legislation to all-out war. One of the last significant events was the passing of the Dawes Act in 1887. What did the Dawes Act mandate?

A. It converted Native American reservation land into separate parcels.
B. It created the states of North Dakota, South Dakota, and Montana.
C. It outlawed gun sales in major cities west of the Mississippi River.
D. It provided American citizenship to all Native Americans.

21. Much of the lore of the West originated not in fact but in fiction. One of the most successful Western authors was Zane Grey. True or False: Zane Grey was born in a town called Zanesville.

ANSWERS

★ ★ ★ ★ ★ ★

19. **Answer: D. 2,500.** Warriors from a number of different Native American nations came together to fight with Sitting Bull against the encroaching soldiers. Custer grossly underestimated the number of warriors encamped at the Little Bighorn River in Montana territory and initiated the attack. Led into battle by Oglala chief Crazy Horse, among others, the warriors easily defeated Custer and his troops.

20. **Answer: A. It converted Native American reservation land into separate parcels.** The Dawes Act provided 160 acres for each Native American family, with the provision that it could not be sold for 25 years. Any excess acreage was sold to pioneers. Although passed with noble intentions, the Dawes Act actually became a continuation of efforts to break up Native American communities and traditions.

21. **Answer: True.** Zanesville, Ohio, was the birthplace for the writer in 1875. Originally a dentist, Zane Grey published his first book at age 29. He went on to create stories of thrilling events in the Wild West, including *Riders of the Purple Sage, The Thundering Herd, Code of the West, West of the Pecos,* and *The Last of the Plainsmen.* Many of his stories were turned into movies.

MILITARY

★ ★ ★ ★ ★ ★ ★ ★ ★

America is blessed with a proud military tradition. Much of the honor and courage of America has been forged in wartime. How is your knowledge of American military history?

1. Francis Scott Key, the author of the American national anthem, "The Star-Spangled Banner," was writing about an actual flag in wartime. During which war did Key write "The Star-Spangled Banner"?

A. The American Revolution
B. The War of 1812
C. The Spanish-American War
D. The Civil War

2. On June 8, 1959, the U.S.S. *Barbero* submarine fired a 36-foot Regulus 1 winged missile at Mayport Auxiliary Station in Florida. Why?

A. The station had been taken over by Korean nationals.
B. It was a demonstration of force to the Communists.
C. The missile needed repair.
D. It was used to deliver mail.

3. In 1947, journalist Walter Lippmann wrote a book whose title added a new term to our national vocabulary. What was its title?

A. *Shell Shock*
B. *The Cold War*
C. *Military Intelligence*
D. *Iron Curtain*

Answers

★ ★ ★ ★ ★ ★ ★

1. Answer: B. The War of 1812. A huge flag—a quarter the size of a modern basketball court—flew over Fort McHenry as it was under siege from British shells. This was a dramatic symbol of the fledgling nation's strength, which seemed unlikely at the time to prevail against the British. Francis Scott Key was being held on a ship in the harbor. After 25 hours of shelling, he awoke to see that the American flag was still flying over the fort. He wrote his stirring poem, originally titled "The Defense of Ft. McHenry," about it.

2. Answer: D. It was used to deliver mail. This was the first recorded use of missile mail, which carried 3,000 letters addressed to President Dwight D. Eisenhower and other government officials.

3. Answer: B. *The Cold War.* Walter Lippmann coined this term to describe the relations between the United States and the Soviet Union after World War II. Unlike traditional wars, it is difficult to mark the exact beginning of the Cold War. Many cite June 5, 1945, when Secretary of State George Marshall laid out a plan to provide massive aid to rebuild war-ravaged Europe. Its roots, however, go further back than that. Diplomatic relations between the United States and the Soviet Union, for instance, did not even exist between 1917 and 1933. The countries briefly became allies in World War II after each was attacked by the Axis in 1941.

QUESTIONS

★ ★ ★ ★ ★ ★ ★

4. During the early years of World War I in Europe, the United States had declared itself neutral to stay out of the war. A few events challenged American neutrality and ultimately contributed to the country's entry into the war in 1917. One such event was the sinking of a luxury passenger liner by German U-boats. What was its name?

A. The *Titanic*
B. The *Maine*
C. The *Lusitania*
D. The *Andrea Doria*

5. Beginning with George Washington, the military hero has always been a fixture of the American landscape. What U.S. general was known by the nickname "Old Rough and Ready"?

A. George Patton
B. Zachary Taylor
C. John J. Pershing
D. Norman Schwarzkopf

6. Born in 1931 to Kentucky sharecroppers, Carl Brashear entered the U.S. Navy and became the first African American member of the Navy's elite diving team. A freak shipboard accident caused him to lose his left leg, but his military career was not yet over. What other first did Brashear attain?

A. He became the first African American submarine commander.
B. He became the first amputee in the White House honor guard.
C. He became the first amputee Navy diver.
D. He became the first Navy adviser in Vietnam.

Answers

★ ★ ★ ★ ★ ★ ★

4. **Answer: C. The *Lusitania*.** The British floating palace carried 1,959 passengers. It had no weapons, but it carried a cargo that was almost entirely made up of contraband, including tons of ammunition. Torpedoed just hours before it was due to arrive in Liverpool, the ship sank in 18 minutes—so quickly that few people could escape. The fatalities included 1,195 passengers, 123 of them American.

5. **Answer: B. Zachary Taylor.** Taylor, who would later be elected the 12th president of the United States in 1848, had fought in the War of 1812 and in campaigns against the Seminoles in Florida during the Black Hawk War (where he earned his nickname). He became a national hero due to his victories in the Mexican-American War.

6. **Answer: C. He became the first amputee Navy diver.** When Carl Brashear lost his leg, he fought to remain on active duty, battling to prove to the Navy that he was as able as any two-legged diver. He continually went against orders meant to aid his recovery, but his determination paid off. He became the first amputee diver in the Navy and went on to serve in the military for years, attaining the rank of Master Diver.

QUESTIONS

★ ★ ★ ★ ★ ★ ★ ★

7. Andrew Jackson's victory over the British in the Battle of New Orleans made him a national hero of the War of 1812. But there was also something else quite notable about this battle. What was it?

A. It was the last use of the U.S. Cavalry.
B. It was fought on seven battlefields.
C. It was the first use of machine guns by U.S. troops.
D. It was fought after the War of 1812 had ended.

8. The term *ace* came into our language during World War I. What was its original military meaning?

A. A British infantry soldier in the trenches
B. A pilot who shot down at least five enemy planes
C. An American soldier in the European theater
D. A German submarine

9. There can be many hardships during wartime, and one can be just as destructive as another. During World War I, for instance, which killed more people: military action or disease?

10. In 1881, according to inventor Hiram Maxim, an acquaintance advised him, "If you wish to make a pile of money, invent something that will enable these Europeans to cut each other's throats with greater facility." Maxim took this advice. What did he invent?

A. The grenade
B. Poison gas
C. The bayonet
D. The machine gun

Answers

★ ★ ★ ★ ★ ★

7. Answer: D. It was fought after the War of 1812 had ended. The Treaty of Ghent was signed to end the war between the United States and England in December 1814, two weeks before the Battle of New Orleans was fought in January of the next year. But it would be another month before news of the war's end reached the state of Louisiana.

8. Answer: B. A pilot who shot down at least five enemy planes. World War I was the world's first real air war, and people spoke about the "flying aces" on both sides of the fighting. This definition can still be found in modern dictionaries. After the war, the word *ace* came to refer to an expert in any field.

9. Answer: Disease. A flu pandemic beginning in 1918, the last year of the war, devastated the world. Estimated fatalities ran from 20 to 40 million people. Half of the world's population was believed to have been infected. In contrast, roughly 18 million people, military and civilian, were lost on both sides due to World War I military action.

10. Answer: D. The machine gun. The weapon, which fed a canvas belt with cartridges into the gun, fired up to 600 rounds per minute. Hiram Maxim first developed a working model in 1885, which was adopted by the British army within a few years.

QUESTIONS

★ ★ ★ ★ ★ ★ ★

11. In 1855, Jefferson Davis, then U.S. secretary of war under President Franklin Pierce (and later president of the Confederacy), was pushing an innovative idea for the military. He convinced Congress to appropriate $30,000 to institute it. What did Davis get for that money?

A. A Southern army
B. The first order of tanks for the military
C. Camels
D. Exclusive use of the railroads in times of military crisis

12. We often think of biological warfare as a 20th-century phenomenon, popularized during World War I, but such tactics have popped up throughout history. True or False: American colonists conducted germ warfare against Native Americans.

13. Just like the rest of American society, the U.S. military has become more inclusive through the years, welcoming a wider variety of people into its ranks. On February 3, 1981, the Air Force Academy dropped its ban on what group of people?

A. People with glasses
B. Homosexuals
C. People with sickle-cell trait
D. Women

Answers

★ ★ ★ ★ ★ ★ ★

11. Answer: C. Camels. Imported from Egypt, the camels were used by Lieutenant Edward Beale to survey a route from Fort Defiance, New Mexico, to eastern California. Beale was enthusiastic about the camel corps, and he ordered 1,000 more camels in 1858. Other soldiers, however, found the beasts difficult to handle, and the experiment ended during the Civil War.

12. Answer: True. General Jeffrey Amherst, the commander-in-chief of the British forces in North America, discussed a plan in 1763 to infect Native Americans with blankets taken from a smallpox ward. It was reported later that year from Fort Pitt in Pennsylvania, "Out of our regard for [two Native American chiefs] we gave them two blankets and a handkerchief out of the smallpox hospital. I hope it will have the desired effect." Smallpox broke out among Native Americans that year and took a heavy toll. Amherst was later made an English lord. Amherst College; Amherst, Massachusetts; and several other U.S. towns bear his name.

13. Answer: C. People with sickle-cell trait. The sickle-cell trait tends to appear predominantly in African Americans. Many people considered the Air Force Academy's ban on people carrying the sickle-cell trait to be a way to legally discriminate against African Americans, so the policy was dropped.

Civil Rights

★★★★★★★★★★★

In 1776, the Declaration of Independence observed that "all men are created equal." What looked good on paper took some time to become reality. The struggle for civil rights throughout American history has been the struggle to make that statement true for everyone regardless of race, religion, or gender. How much do you know about the highlights of this cause?

1. It can be argued that African Americans have had the most difficult road to travel in attaining their civil rights. A number of organizations have appeared over the years to help achieve those rights. The Congress of Racial Equality is one example. Who founded this group in 1942?

A. Roy Wilkins
B. Medgar Evers
C. Martin Luther King, Jr.
D. James Farmer

2. The Liberty Bell in Philadelphia is famous throughout the world as a symbol of American freedom. But it was not always known by that name. True or False: The Liberty Bell received its name as a symbol for the freedom of black slaves.

3. The Supreme Court's 1973 decision in the case of *Roe* v. *Wade* is a landmark of modern law, making abortion legal throughout the United States. True or False: Before *Roe* v. *Wade*, abortion was illegal throughout the United States.

Answers

★ ★ ★ ★ ★ ★

1. Answer: D. James Farmer. The Congress of Racial Equality, often called CORE, was formed to fight segregation with peaceful protests. On January 15, 1998, after a four-year letter-writing campaign by people like NAACP chairman Julian Bond, President Bill Clinton awarded Farmer the Medal of Freedom, the nation's highest civilian honor.

2. Answer: True. The same bell hung in the Philadephia statehouse from the time when Pennsylvania was still an English colony, but it had never been given any particular name. For some of the time it wasn't even considered significant—in 1828 Philadelphia tried to sell it for scrap, but there were no takers. The first time anyone called it the Liberty Bell was in a book by that same name distributed at the Massachusetts Anti-Slavery Fair in 1839.

3. Answer: False. Until the mid-19th century, abortion was a legal and accepted practice, but between 1860 and 1880 every state passed laws criminalizing the procedure. It remained illegal for almost a century (although it wasn't usually questioned legally unless the mother died), but even before the 1973 *Roe* decision, some states had rescinded their laws and others had loosened restrictions. What *Roe* v. *Wade* did was establish a fundamental right to abortion at the federal level.

QUESTIONS

★ ★ ★ ★ ★ ★ ★

4. On March 30, 1870, the 15th Amendment of the U.S. Constitution went into effect. The next day, Thomas Peterson-Mundy of Perth Amboy, New Jersey, became the first to take advantage of its authority. What did he do?

A. Ran for office
B. Enlisted in the army
C. Bought alcohol
D. Voted

5. For much of American history, Congress remained a man's domain. As the 20th century progressed, however, more and more women were elected to Congress. A lawyer was elected to the House of Representatives in 1970 and became the founder and chair of the National Women's Political Caucus. Who was she?

A. Gloria Steinem
B. Bella Abzug
C. Geraldine Ferraro
D. Betty Friedan

6. Activism for equal rights for gays and lesbians really came into its own on June 28, 1969, when New York City police raided a bar in Greenwich Village. What was the name of that bar?

A. The Bull and Finch
B. Babylon
C. New York Men's Club
D. Stonewall Inn

7. The 20th Amendment to the Constitution, ratified in 1920, gave women the right to vote. But the laws have been fluid throughout American history. True or False: Women in the state of New Jersey had the right to vote in 1776.

Answers

★ ★ ★ ★ ★ ★

4. Answer: D. Voted. The 15th Amendment extended the vote to freed slaves, and Thomas Peterson-Mundy was the first to take advantage of it. He voted in a special election for ratification of a city charter. The charter was adopted, and Peterson-Mundy was appointed to the committee to revise it.

5. Answer: B. Bella Abzug. Abzug's aggressive approach to her causes earned her the nicknames "Battling Bella," "Hurricane Bella," and "Mother Courage." She served three terms in the House and went on to write a column for *Ms. Magazine*.

6. Answer: D. Stonewall Inn. During the 1960s, police in all cities regularly raided places where gays and lesbians gathered. When the Stonewall Inn was raided, however, 200 homosexual patrons refused to go quietly. A 45-minute riot ensued, and the riot repeated on succeeding nights. Gay activists credit the event as the birth of the gay rights movement.

7. Answer: True. The 1776 New Jersey constitution said that, regardless of gender, "all inhabitants" with 50 pounds to their name could vote. Many women did not exercise the right until a hotly contested election in 1797, when 75 women came en masse to vote for their preferred candidate. After that, candidates started taking groups of women to the polls. In one 1807 election, both sides battled to get women to the polls. There were even reports of boys coming in women's clothing. Later that year, New Jersey lawmakers barred women from voting.

QUESTIONS

★ ★ ★ ★ ★ ★ ★

8. Prior to the Civil War, settlers in a U.S. territory seeking statehood could decide whether to be a free or a slave state. When Kansas sought statehood, abolitionists formed organizations to encourage members to move to the territory in order to stack the deck in their favor. One of the most successful was the Emigrant Aid Company. Who was both its treasurer and a large contributor?

A. Benjamin Franklin
B. John Quincy Adams
C. Amos Lawrence
D. William Lloyd Garrison

9. In 1961, to raise the profile of the civil rights issue, the Congress of Racial Equality held something they called Freedom Rides. What were they?

A. A group of white housewives who drove African Americans during the Montgomery bus boycotts
B. Bus trips in which multiracial groups stopped and ate at segregated restaurants
C. Marches along the routes of segregated buses
D. Busloads of people trying to integrate schools

10. In 1920 Roger Baldwin founded an organization to champion civil and Constitutional rights through the due process of law. What is the name of this group?

A. National Organization for Women
B. The Freedom Institute
C. United Way
D. American Civil Liberties Union

ANSWERS

★ ★ ★ ★ ★ ★

8. **Answer: C. Amos Lawrence.** The city of Lawrence, Kansas, one of the few American cities founded for purely political reasons, was named in his honor. It became an important stop on the underground railroad, and as pro-slavery groups tried to send their own settlers, it became the site of a number of bloody skirmishes.

9. **Answer: B. Bus trips in which multiracial groups stopped and ate at segregated restaurants.** A group of African American and white activists took two public bus lines and, at each stop, they sat together in segregated restaurants. In some cities the riders were attacked. By the time they reached the state of Mississippi, most of the participants had been arrested for breaking various segregation laws.

10. **Answer: D. American Civil Liberties Union.** The ACLU initiates test cases and provides legal assistance in cases already before the court. Also involved in founding the group were Helen Keller, Jane Addams, and future Supreme Court justice Felix Frankfurter. One of the ACLU's most famous cases was the "Scopes Monkey Trial." It has fought against censorship laws and defended a variety of people and groups ranging from Jehovah's Witnesses, who refused to allow their children to say the Pledge of Allegiance to the flag in school, to Lieutenant Colonel Oliver North. The ACLU currently has about 275,000 members.

Questions

★ ★ ★ ★ ★ ★ ★

11. In 1939 African American opera singer Marian Anderson was denied permission to perform in Constitution Hall. Run by the Daughters of the American Revolution (DAR), the hall had a policy at the time of denying its use to African Americans. Anderson did something in response to the situation. What was it?

A. Staged a sit-in
B. Performed on the steps of the Lincoln Memorial
C. Marched on Congress
D. Sued the DAR and won

12. Poet and author Helen Hunt Jackson published a book, *A Century of Dishonor*, in 1881. She considered its subject so important that she paid to have copies delivered to every member of Congress. What was the subject of the book?

A. Slavery
B. U.S. Native American policies
C. The role of women in government
D. Treatment of migrant workers

13. The first woman to run for president of the United States did so against Ulysses S. Grant in 1872, 48 years before women had the right to vote. She championed not only women's suffrage, but also free love and mystical socialism. Who was she?

A. Geraldine Ferraro
B. Susan B. Anthony
C. Victoria Woodhull
D. Jane Addams

ANSWERS

★ ★ ★ ★ ★ ★

11. **Answer: B. Performed on the steps of the Lincoln Memorial.** Marian Anderson was invited to perform on Easter morning of 1939, for any and all who cared to hear her. The live audience numbered 75,000, with millions listening on the radio. In the summer of that year, she was honored with the NAACP's Spingarn Medal for "her magnificent dignity as a human being."

12. **Answer: B. U.S. Native American policies.** The release of *A Century of Dishonor* led to Helen Hunt Jackson's appointment by the Department of the Interior the next year to investigate the condition of Native Americans in California. She offered a report in July 1883, but it made no impression on the government.

13. **Answer: C. Victoria Woodhull.** One of America's greatest characters, Woodhull, born in 1838, grew up in her family's traveling fortune-telling medicine show. Business tycoon Cornelius Vanderbilt helped her start a successful stockbrokerage firm, but she was also interested in socialism and the concept of communal marriage and property. In the 1870s she and her sister published a weekly magazine that advocated equal rights for women. That led to her becoming the presidential candidate of the Equal Rights Party. She was in jail on election day, however, charged with sending obscene materials through the mail.

Questions

★ ★ ★ ★ ★ ★ ★

14. In the first half of the 20th century, the rights of California farm workers were mostly ignored. That began to change after World War II, as organizers and unions made their presence felt. One activist founded the National Farm Workers Association in 1962, which merged with the Agricultural Workers Organizing Committee, AFL-CIO, to form the United Farm Workers of America, AFL-CIO. Who was this union organizer?

A. Cesar Chavez
B. Joe Hill
C. Jimmy Hoffa
D. John L. Lewis

15. In 1839 Africans being taken as slaves to Cuba on the ship *Amistad* mutinied and seized the ship. Off of Long Island, a U.S. warship boarded the vessel and towed it to Connecticut, where began a drawn-out legal battle to determine whether the Africans should be freed or returned to Africa. What American president represented the enslaved Africans before the Supreme Court?

A. John Quincy Adams
B. Martin Van Buren
C. Abraham Lincoln
D. Thomas Jefferson

16. In February 1960, four African American college students in Greensboro, North Carolina, gained national attention with a sit-in. What was their goal?

A. Better representation in colleges
B. To integrate lunch counters
C. To support the Montgomery bus boycott
D. An end to the Vietnam War

Answers

★ ★ ★ ★ ★ ★ ★

14. **Answer: A. Cesar Chavez.** A sincere advocate of nonviolence, Chavez was tireless in his efforts to improve conditions for farm workers and their families. He organized what became known as *"La Causa"* through boycotts, strikes, and personal fasts.

15. **Answer: A. John Quincy Adams.** A lower court ordered President Martin Van Buren to release the Africans, but the president didn't comply. That's when 74-year-old former President Adams, a staunch abolitionist later in life, took the case. He argued that, based on the Declaration of Independence, the mutineers were free persons whose actions to defend themselves were justified. He won.

16. **Answer: B. To integrate lunch counters.** The group sat at a Woolworth store lunch counter and waited to be served, returning day after day as the store refused. Members of the Nashville Student Movement in Tennessee joined in this cause, staging sit-ins at lunch counters in their city. In May, lunch counters in Nashville began serving African American customers, and the Greensburo Woolworth's served its first meal to an African American in July.

Heroes and Villains

★★★★★★★★★★★★★★★

The good and the bad, the rich and the poor, the haves and the have-nots. Across the years of American history, there have always been individuals who rise above the norm and seize the moment—some for better, others for worse. The people highlighted in this chapter accomplished something extraordinary, whether for good or for bad.

1. There are a few differences between English written by Americans and English written by the British. It is largely thanks to this lexicographer that Americans do not spell *color* or *humor* with a *u*. Who was he?

A. Daniel Webster
B. Noah Webster
C. Rand McNally
D. Ernest Funk

2. This gunslinger was buried in Deadwood, South Dakota, beside old friend Wild Bill Hickok in 1903.

A. Belle Starr
B. Wyatt Earp
C. John Wesley Hardin
D. Calamity Jane

3. He's a man who is remembered for a number of things, but maybe not so much for his name. What does the *J* in the name of former FBI director J. Edgar Hoover stand for?

A. James
B. Jeffery
C. John
D. Josiah

Answers

★ ★ ★ ★ ★ ★

1. **Answer: B. Noah Webster.** Webster's 1828 *American Dictionary of the English Language* established set forms of spelling and pronunciation in the United States. He advocated spelling reform and was largely responsible for the differences that exist between American and British spelling today.

2. **Answer: D. Calamity Jane.** Dressed as a man and toting a gun, Martha Jane Canary roamed the West until she landed in the Black Hills of South Dakota. There she finally settled. She was an excellent shot, and a number of stories of courage and heroism grew up around her. She may have been successful at shooting, but Calamity Jane was a calamity at marriage (she went to the altar 12 times) and at finances (she died penniless).

3. **Answer: C. John.** John Edgar Hoover was named acting director of the Bureau of Investigation (it wasn't called the Federal Bureau of Investigation until 1935) in 1924 and was confirmed director seven months later. He ran the FBI until his death in 1972. Among his accomplishments were the establishment of the world's largest fingerprint file, a scientific detection lab, and the FBI National Academy. He also used the organization's secret files to his benefit, blackmailing politicians to secure his powerful position.

Questions

★ ★ ★ ★ ★ ★ ★

4. It could be said that corporate titan John D. Rockefeller built an empire in the early years of the 20th century. What is the industry most closely associated with Rockefeller?

A. Steel
B. Railroads
C. Banking
D. Oil

5. A written language is often considered a building block of civilization. Who was the only person to singlehandedly invent a written language and bring literacy to a culture?

A. Booker T. Washington
B. Benjamin Franklin
C. Sequoyah
D. Annie Sullivan

6. Until the development and widespread availability of vaccines, people were terrified of disease. It didn't take much for hysteria to turn into panic. One disease that could become an epidemic was typhoid fever. True or False: Typhoid Mary was a real person.

7. Every year the city of Farmington, Maine, celebrates "Chester Greenwood Day" in honor of a man who did something to improve life in that state. What did he do?

A. He singlehandedly defeated a British regiment.
B. He was the first to fish for lobster.
C. He proposed that the area split from Massachusetts to become its own state.
D. He invented earmuffs.

ANSWERS

★ ★ ★ ★ ★ ★

4. Answer: D. Oil. While the Rockefeller patriarch had fingers in many fields, he dominated the oil industry to such an extent that his Standard Oil Company of New Jersey was dissolved in 1911 in a historic antitrust suit.

5. Answer: C. Sequoyah. The son of a Cherokee woman and a Virginia trader, Sequoyah was fascinated by settlers' books. He divided the sounds of spoken Cherokee into 86 syllables and designed a symbol for each. In 1821 he introduced the script to his leaders, who mastered it in a week and gave him permission to teach their people.

6. Answer: True. In the early 1900s, Mary Mallon, who carried typhoid fever, cooked in rich summer homes and kitchens. Her meals were delicious... and deadly. Wherever she worked, people came down with the disease. By the time anyone made the connection, she had infected at least 26 people. Mallon refused to stop cooking, and she was arrested. Quarantined for years, she was released in 1910 when she agreed not to work as a cook again. She lied. Under another name, Mallon took a job cooking in a hospital, causing a new typhoid outbreak.

7. Answer: D. He invented earmuffs. When he turned 15 in 1873, Chester Greenwood received ice skates. To keep his ears from freezing while he skated in the cold wind, he rigged up some beaver fur and wire, which he called "ear mufflers." He patented his invention in 1877 and started manufacturing them the following year. The citizens of Farmington are so grateful for the warmth that they have a Chester Greenwood parade every December.

QUESTIONS

★ ★ ★ ★ ★ ★ ★

8. The expression "rarer than a Button Gwinnett" actually refers to a real person. Who was Button Gwinnett?

A. The author of the U.S. Constitution
B. A signer of the Declaration of Independence
C. Vice-president under John Adams
D. The designer of the first presidential mansion

9. In 1900 a woman named Carry Nation did something for the first time. She would repeat this activity until her death in 1911, gaining national notoriety. What did Carry Nation do?

A. Showed up at the polls to vote
B. Sang on stage
C. Robbed a bank
D. Smashed up a bar

10. The first female attorney in America was Margaret Brent of Maryland. She began her work as a lawyer when a court appointed her attorney for the proprietor of her brother-in-law's estate. In what year did she first practice law?

A. 1647
B. 1747
C. 1847
D. 1947

ANSWERS

★ ★ ★ ★ ★ ★ ★

8. Answer: B. A signer of the Declaration of Independence. After Georgia representative Button Gwinnett signed the Declaration of Independence, he didn't have time to sign much else—he was killed in a duel less than a year later. Due to his untimely passing, the name Button Gwinnett became synonymous with scarcity, as in the expression "rarer than a Button Gwinnett." The expression has itself become rare and refers to the value of a Gwinnett autograph, which fetches as much as $150,000.

9. Answer: D. Smashed up a bar. After her first husband drank himself to death, Carry Nation went on a crusade. The Kansas woman smashed up her first barroom with bricks wrapped in newspaper—she later became famous for wielding a metal hatchet. She attacked more than 20 saloons in the next year and was arrested more than 30 times. She paid her fines by selling souvenir hatchets. She called men "nicotine-soaked, beer-besmeared, whiskey-greased, red-eyed devils."

10. Answer: A. 1647. Margaret Brent, the first woman to hold a land grant in Maryland, called her 70½ acres "Sisters Freehold." There she raised up a troop of soldiers to help Leonard Cecil Calvert in an armed dispute. Afterward, Calvert, who according to some reports was her brother-in-law, appointed her executor of his estate. She took charge of the estate upon his death in May 1647 and received a court appointment as attorney for the proprietor.

Questions

★ ★ ★ ★ ★ ★ ★

11. P. T. Barnum was, without a doubt, one of the great showmen of American history. His very name invokes "the greatest show on earth." True or False: P. T. Barnum invented the modern circus.

12. This Boston school teacher began a crusade in 1842 to get better treatment for mentally ill patients, most of whom were housed in jails. Due to this individual's efforts, by 1880 only 397 of 91,959 mentally ill persons—0.4 percent—were jailed. What was this reformer's name?

A. Louisa May Alcott
B. Dorothea Dix
C. Margaret Sanger
D. Rachel Carson

13. This first-term senator leapt to national prominence after a February 1950 speech in which he claimed that 205 Communists had infiltrated the State Department. For the next few years he was in the spotlight for his anti-communist crusade. Who was he?

A. John F. Kennedy
B. Joseph McCarthy
C. Richard Nixon
D. Barry Goldwater

Answers

★ ★ ★ ★ ★ ★ ★

11. **Answer: False.** Phineas Taylor Barnum did not invent the modern circus. In fact, he did not even become a circus promoter until 1870 when he was 60. Along with James A. Bailey, however, Barnum did give the circus much of its pizzazz and popularity. One of the most famous quotes attributed to Barnum is "There's a sucker born every minute." The only thing is, he never made that statment. It was actually uttered by a business rival, complaining that Barnum had maneuvered his audience away from him. Sucker!

12. **Answer: B. Dorothea Dix.** Dix wrote a passionate letter to the Massachusetts legislature, vividly describing the plight of the impoverished mentally ill. Later, as she campaigned to build a mental institution in New Jersey, Dix wrote that jailing the mentally ill made as much sense as jailing someone for contracting tuberculosis. She continued to write and meet with legislators and health officials, whom she convinced to open 30 psychiatric hospitals for the indigent.

13. **Answer: B. Joseph McCarthy.** McCarthy held up a "list" of "card-carrying Communists" during his speech, but he later had to admit there was no such list. That still didn't stop the hunt for Communists. McCarthy never proved a case, but his accusations were enough to cost many their jobs. After hearings on charges of subversion by U.S. Army officers were nationally televised in 1954, public opinion turned against him. He was censured by the Senate for unbecoming conduct on December 2, 1954, ending the era of McCarthyism.

QUESTIONS

★ ★ ★ ★ ★ ★ ★

14. During the Civil War, this former schoolteacher became known as the "angel of the battlefield." She later founded the American Red Cross. What was this woman's name?

A. Florence Nightingale
B. Clara Barton
C. Mary Baker Eddy
D. Emily Dickinson

15. In 1883 it was discovered that an elusive criminal who robbed stagecoaches and mailboxes was actually a highly respected mining engineer named Charles E. Bolton. What was his outlaw name?

A. Jesse James
B. The Sundance Kid
C. Billy the Kid
D. Black Bart

16. The American newspaper business has always been competitive, but from time to time a dominant publishing magnate comes to the fore. One example was a man who, by 1925, owned newspapers in every section of the United States. What was his name?

A. Joseph Pulitzer
B. Charles Foster Kane
C. Frank Ernest Gannett
D. William Randolph Hearst

ANSWERS

★ ★ ★ ★ ★ ★

14. **Answer: B. Clara Barton.** Barton organized an agency to obtain and distribute supplies for wounded Civil War soldiers. At President Abraham Lincoln's request, she also set up a bureau of records to help find the missing. While she traveled in Europe, the Franco-German War broke out. Instead of returning home, Barton distributed relief supplies to war victims. Her work with the International Red Cross led her, in 1881, to establish the American National Red Cross. One change made to the American Red Cross's constitution was that it would distribute relief in times of natural disaster as well as wartime.

15. **Answer: D. Black Bart.** The infamous highwayman gained notoriety by leaving behind rhymes signed "Black Bart, Po8." His true identity was discovered when a laundry mark was found on a handkerchief dropped near the scene of a robbery in Calaveras County, California. The name Bolton itself may have been an alias, as his last name was variously reported as Boles and Bowles.

16. **Answer: D. William Randolph Hearst.** Hearst built the nation's largest newspaper chain with a blend of investigative reporting and sensationalism. He was so influential that his newspapers' coverage of Cuba actually helped cause the Spanish-American War. At his height in 1935 he owned 28 major newspapers; 18 magazines; and several radio stations, movie companies, and news services. He failed to cut his extravagant lifestyle back during the Great Depression, and his fortune began to falter. By 1940 he had lost personal control of his media empire.

BUSINESS AND THE ECONOMY

★ ★ ★ ★ ★ ★ ★ ★ ★ ★ ★ ★ ★ ★ ★ ★

The wizards of Wall Street and barons of business have certainly done their part to shape America. Stories of financiers, retailers, and manufacturers are all a part of the American dream. Find out if your business knowledge is "right on the money."

1. If there's a single place that defines business in America, it's Wall Street in New York City. How did Wall Street get its name?

A. It was named for an early resident, Frederick Wall.
B. There used to be an actual wall there.
C. It was an imaginary division between two sections of the city.
D. *Wall* is an ancient Dutch word for *bank*.

2. The gas crisis in the 1970s was not the nation's first fuel shortage. Another energy crisis hit in the 1840s, forcing up prices of a common fuel. What was this fuel?

A. Coal
B. Turpentine
C. Wood
D. Whale oil

3. Leaders of business seek immortality as much as anyone else, and they sometimes achieve it by giving their name to a company that outlasts them. Which of the following businesses was named for its founder?

A. L. L. Bean
B. T. J. Maxx
C. J. Crew
D. Arm & Hammer

Answers

★ ★ ★ ★ ★ ★

1. Answer: B. There used to be an actual wall there. The narrow street in lower Manhattan that is the center of the U.S. financial world takes its name from a wall built by Dutch colonists in 1653 to defend the city against an expected attack by Native Americans.

2. Answer: D. Whale oil. In the 1840s whale oil was burned for lights and useful for the lubrication of machines. By the 1850s, despite a whaling fleet of more than 700 vessels, prices had leapt to $2 a gallon, and Americans started looking for alternatives, such as coal oil and petroleum.

3. Answer: A. L. L. Bean. The mail-order company was named for Leon Leonwood Bean, a hunter who sold boots through the mail. The name *J. Crew* was invented by founder Emily Woods; *Crew* comes from the sport crewing, and *J.* just sounded good with *Crew*. *T. J. Maxx* was entirely fabricated. Despite rumors to the contrary, Arm & Hammer baking soda did not take its name from industrialist Armand Hammer. The name came from the logo, which portrays the arm of the god Vulcan.

QUESTIONS

★ ★ ★ ★ ★ ★ ★

4. Mahatma Gandhi is said to have called this machine "one of the few useful things ever invented." Admiral Richard Byrd found it so useful that he carted six all the way to the Antarctic. What was it?

A. The Singer sewing machine
B. The L. C. Smith Typewriter
C. The Gillette safety razor
D. The Davy lantern

5. Two brothers developed a successful fast-food restaurant in San Bernardino, California. But when they sold the restaurant to Ray Kroc, they gave up the right to use their own name on a business. What was their last name?

A. Hardee
B. McDonald
C. Denny
D. Sanders

6. In 1930 Herman G. Weinberg, a German immigrant to New York, pioneered a totally new career field, something that had never been done before. How did Weinberg start making money?

A. Writing movie subtitles
B. Mass-producing beer
C. Repairing televisions
D. Selling business advice to women

ANSWERS

★ ★ ★ ★ ★ ★

4. **Answer: A. The Singer sewing machine.** Isaac Singer did not invent the sewing machine, but those that had existed prior to 1850 were bulky and unreliable. In 1851 Singer received a patent for his version. Singer's patent attracted the attention of Elias Howe, who had patented an earlier sewing machine in 1846. Howe sued and, after a long court battle, won. Singer was ordered to pay Howe $15,000 in back royalties. Howe was further entitled to $5 for every sewing machine sold in America.

5. **Answer: B. McDonald.** Richard and Maurice McDonald opened their fast-food shop shortly after World War II. Ray Kroc convinced them to franchise it, and in 1961 he bought them out completely. Although Kroc bought the McDonald's name, the brothers' original restaurant wasn't included in the deal. The McDonald brothers stayed in the fast-food business, but they had to rename their restaurant. Kroc put a McDonald's just a block away from the brothers' business, and eight years later they decided to sell that, too.

6. **Answer: A. Writing movie subtitles.** Before talking pictures came along, it was little or no problem for theaters to present movies from around the world. A few title cards might need to be translated, but that was it. After sound, however, it became much more difficult. How could the American audience understand what the characters were saying? The answer was subtitles. Herman G. Weinberg wrote titles for the first subtitled movie in the United States, *Two Hearts in Waltz Time*. Over the next 40 years he subtitled a record 450 foreign-language films.

QUESTIONS

★ ★ ★ ★ ★ ★ ★

7. In 1882 a pair of seasoned journalists set up an office in a Wall Street basement and started delivering financial news in handwritten bulletins. This operation evolved, 14 years later, into *The Wall Street Journal*. The reporters' first names were Charles and Edward, but they're better known for their last names. What were they?

A. Standard and Poor
B. Smith and Corona
C. Dow and Jones
D. Johnson and Johnson

8. Philip Danforth Armour, of Armour meat products fame, made his fortune gambling on hog futures. He sold futures to New York traders at $40 a barrel, certain he would make a profit. The fall of the Confederacy and a new invention, he predicted, would cause pork prices to fall, allowing him to fill orders below that price. On what invention did Armour stake his future?

A. The assembly line
B. The refrigerated train car
C. Electric cutting knives
D. Cellophane

9. American icons can be established in a number of different ways. They can sometimes come from the government and politics, or from movies and TV. Sometimes they come from business. What famous landmark began life as an advertisement?

A. The Statue of Liberty
B. The Hollywood sign
C. Mount Rushmore
D. The Seattle Space Needle

Answers

★ ★ ★ ★ ★ ★ ★

7. **Answer: C. Dow and Jones.** Charles Henry Dow and Edward D. Jones published their first Dow Jones Industrial Average, then a daily composite of 12 "smokestack" companies that produced coal, leather, cotton, and sugar, on May 26, 1896. The first publication of an average comparable to today's industrial stocks was on October 1, 1928. The Dow closed that day at 240.01.

8. **Answer: B. The refrigerated train car.** Shortly after the Civil War, the first refrigerated railroad car had been built. This kept meat products from spoiling and allowed farmers to expand the market for those products. After Philip Armour sold hog futures for $40 a barrel, as he predicted, prices fell, and he was able to fill orders with pork bought at only $18 a barrel.

9. **Answer: B. The Hollywood sign.** In 1923 a real estate developer erected a giant sign reading "Hollywoodland" to advertise a new housing development by that name. The sign was planned to last for a year and a half. A few years later the "land" part of the sign fell down and was never replaced. The company behind the housing development may be gone, but the Hollywood sign is known the world over.

QUESTIONS

★ ★ ★ ★ ★ ★ ★

10. Before cars made traveling to the store easy, much of the retail business in the United States was done through the mail. Who was responsible for America's first mail order catalog?

A. Richard Warren Sears
B. Alvah Curtis Roebuck
C. Aaron Montgomery Ward
D. Joseph Spiegel

11. A major step forward in industrial production came with the development of the assembly line, which allowed much greater efficiency in producing and assembling goods. Where was the first assembly line used in America?

A. Henry Ford's assembly plant
B. A Cincinnati slaughterhouse
C. A Boston milliner shop
D. Ransom E. Olds's auto assembly plant

12. True or False: When the Pilgrims arrived at Plymouth in 1620, they established a type of communist economy.

Answers

★ ★ ★ ★ ★ ★

10. **Answer: C. Aaron Montgomery Ward.** In 1875 Ward got tired of life on the road as a traveling salesman. With $1,600 he and two partners filled a warehouse with goods and sent farmers a catalog of items they could purchase by mail. Ward's "Wish Book," as it came to be known, predated that of Richard Sears and Alvah Roebuck by 14 years.

11. **Answer: B. A Cincinnati slaughterhouse.** In the 1850s Cincinnati was the center of pork production, where a highly organized system of moving pig carcasses was developed. In 1860 Wilson, Eggleston and Company installed an overhead track to speed up the process. This idea traveled to Chicago, where it was adapted to the slaughterhouses. It was here that Henry Ford got his inspiration for the assembly line.

12. **Answer: True.** Although it would be more than 200 years before Karl Marx wrote *The Communist Manifesto* outlining these economic ideas, the Pilgrims of Plymouth Bay Colony adopted ideas of communal ownership and agricultural production for their new society. They finally discovered, to their disappointment, that people were not willing to work hard enough for the common good. When every family was responsible for raising its own agriculture, the amount of production increased dramatically.

QUESTIONS

★ ★ ★ ★ ★ ★ ★ ★

13. In the 1840s "rich as Astor" was a common expression of wealth. Astor family money helped fund the Metropolitan Museum of Art and Trinity Church Wall Street in New York. The Waldorf-Astoria hotel was built by members of the family, and cities in New York and Oregon were named for them. How did John Jacob Astor make his original fortune?

A. Whaling
B. Guns and amunition
C. Fur trading
D. Oil

14. No one can deny that sweets and desserts are part of American life. Immigrants from around the world have brought delicacies from their homelands to this country. True or False: German chocolate cake comes from Germany.

15. In 1919 and 1920, a businessman attracted thousands of Bostonians to invest with his firm, many of whom had never invested before. Altogether they sank $15 million into International Postal Union coupons. It was later revealed, however, that there had never been any postal coupons. Instead, the man had used money from the later investors to pay earlier investors. What was his name?

A. Charles Dow
B. Charles Ponzi
C. Boss Tweed
D. Elderbridge Gerry

Answers

★ ★ ★ ★ ★ ★

13. **Answer: C. Fur trading.** John Jacob Astor, an immigrant from Waldorf, Germany, was one of the country's first self-made millionaires. He founded the American Fur Company in 1786, and by 1794 he controlled much of the beaver trade in the far west.

14. **Answer: False.** The German chocolate cake actually takes its name from one of the main ingredients, Baker's German's Sweet Chocolate. The chocolate was named for Samuel German, who developed the sweet chocolate in 1852 as an employee of the Massachusetts-based company Baker's Chocolate.

15. **Answer: B. Charles Ponzi.** Investment strategies such as this, in which later investors pay off the investment of the first investors, have since been dubbed "Ponzi schemes." Ponzi served five years in federal prison for his conniving, but he never gave up his fraudulent ways and returned to jail frequently. He finally left the country and wound up in Brazil, where he died almost broke.

WORLD WAR II

★ ★ ★ ★ ★ ★ ★ ★ ★ ★ ★ ★

In the early 1940s, war raged in Europe and in the Pacific. Few countries were able to avoid being drawn into the conflict. Find out what you remember about the reasons, the battles, the people, the places, and the aftermath of World War II.

1. During the Battle of the Bulge in 1944, German forces surrounded the pivotal French town of Bastogne. They called for American forces to surrender, but General Anthony C. McAuliffe, commanding officer of the 101st Airborne Division, which was protecting the town, responded with a one-word answer. What was it?

A. "Nein!"
B. "Nope!"
C. "Nuts!"
D. "Never!"

2. What future U.S. president was shot down over Iwo Jima as a World War II navy pilot?

A. Ronald Reagan
B. George H.W. Bush
C. Gerald Ford
D. John F. Kennedy

3. The expression "Roger Wilco" originated during World War II. Where did it come from?

A. It was the name of a pilot named Roger Wilco.
B. It was the name of the military unit that first used it.
C. It was an abbreviation for "received, will comply."
D. It meant nothing but was intended to confuse the enemy listening in.

ANSWERS

★ ★ ★ ★ ★ ★

1. **Answer: C. "Nuts!"** Seriously outnumbered by Nazi troops, the American soldiers proved tough and ready, holding them off for six days. The 101st was relieved by General George Patton's Third Army on the day after Christmas. The Battle of the Bulge proved to be the final German offensive of the war.

2. **Answer: B. George H. W. Bush.** On September 24, 1944, Bush and two crewmen flew a bombing run over the Pacific. Their aircraft was hit by anti-aircraft fire before it reached the target, but Bush continued on. After releasing his payload, he turned back toward the aircraft carrier. The aircraft he was flying was too badly damaged, however, and couldn't make it. He bailed out over the Pacific, the only member of the crew to survive. After treading water in the ocean for about three hours, Bush was rescued by the U.S. submarine *Finback*. He was later awarded the Distinguished Flying Cross.

3. **Answer: C. It was an abbreviation for "received, will comply."** During World War II *Roger* was the word in the phonetic alphabet that stood for the letter *R*. Pilots used it as a sort of shorthand to mean "received." *Wilco* is short for "will comply." Later the phonetic alphabet used by the American military was changed. *Romeo* is now used for the letter *R*.

Questions

★ ★ ★ ★ ★ ★ ★

4. On March 6, 1941, an entertainer known for the song "Thanks for the Memory" performed for troops at the March Field Airbase in California. He would go on to entertain troops wherever they were stationed during World War II and subsequent conflicts. Who was he?

A. Bing Crosby
B. Bob Hope
C. Milton Berle
D. Fred Astaire

5. Why is the U.S.S. *Reuben James* significant to World War II?

A. It carried the atomic bomb to its port of departure.
B. It was the lead ship in the D-Day invasion of Normandy.
C. It was the first U.S. warship sunk in World War II.
D. It was where the Japanese signed their surrender.

6. True or False: Beginning in 1931, a decade before the Japanese attack on Pearl Harbor, every graduate of the Japanese Naval Academy had to answer the following question as part of the final exam: "How would you carry out a surprise attack on Pearl Harbor?"

7. During World War II, the marines brought in a special group to devise a code the Japanese could not crack. Who made up this group of people?

A. Japanese-Americans
B. Mathematicians
C. Navajos
D. Visually impaired students

ANSWERS

★ ★ ★ ★ ★ ★ ★

4. Answer: B. Bob Hope. His theme song, "Thanks for the Memory," first appeared in the 1938 movie *The Big Broadcast*. After television came along, Hope would tape his military shows for TV specials. He continued to entertain U.S. troops stationed throughout the world. He claimed that his 1972 tour in Vietnam would be his "last Christmas show," but that distinction actually goes to his 1990 show in Saudi Arabia during the Gulf War. He has been rewarded with both a U.S. naval ship and an Air Force aircraft named after him. In 1997 Congress made Hope an Honorary Veteran, a new title that had never before been bestowed.

5. Answer: C. It was the first U.S. warship sunk in World War II. On October 30, 1941, five weeks before Pearl Harbor, the destroyer U.S.S. *Reuben James* was dispatched to convoy duty 600 miles off the coast of Iceland. A German U-boat torpedoed and sunk the *Reuben James*, killing 100 American sailors.

6. Answer: True. Believe it or not, there are a number of reports that this is true. There is no record of whether or not any of the cadets' answers were used in planning the actual attack.

7. Answer: C. Navajos. Navajo is an oral language spoken by few outsiders. The Navajo Code Talkers used ordinary Navajo words combined with several hundred new words coined for the mission. The Code Talkers' efforts helped the marines take Iwo Jima.

QUESTIONS

★ ★ ★ ★ ★ ★ ★

8. Her real name was Iva Ikuko Toguri D'Aquino, and she was known for the sexy voice and bright tone of her radio broadcasts. By what name was she known to millions?

A. Tokyo Rose
B. Mata Hari
C. Rosie the Riveter
D. Saigon Sally

9. He was World War II's most decorated soldier. This Congressional Medal of Honor winner went on to star in several big budget movies. One of his pictures was the story of his own life, the 1955 film *To Hell and Back*. Who was this soldier?

A. Ronald Reagan
B. Audie Murphy
C. James Cagney
D. John Wayne

10. What was the only single U.S. sea engagement in which five brothers were killed?

A. Battle of Guadalcanal
B. Battle of Midway
C. Battle of Britain
D. Invasion of Normandy

11. The total cost of World War II, including veterans' benefits and interest on debts, was about $560 billion. Which of the following wars was more expensive to the United States?

A. Revolutionary War
B. Spanish-American War
C. Vietnam War
D. None of the above

Answers

★ ★ ★ ★ ★ ★

8. **Answer: A. Tokyo Rose.** An American citizen with Japanese parents, she held a degree from UCLA and found herself visiting a sick relative in Japan when war broke out. She joined the Japanese Broadcasting Company and was trained by an American prisoner of war to broadcast Japanese propaganda in an appealing, cheery voice. In 1948 she was tried by the United States and sentenced to 10 years in prison and fined $10,000 for treason.

9. **Answer: B. Audie Murphy.** A 1945 *Life* magazine cover featured Murphy as the most decorated GI of World War II. James Cagney took him under his wing and taught him to act. *To Hell and Back* was based on Murphy's best-selling autobiography. That film held the record as Universal Studio's highest grossing movie for 20 years until the release of Steven Spielberg's *Jaws*.

10. **Answer: A. Battle of Guadalcanal.** On November 13, 1942, a Japanese submarine sank the U.S.S. *Juneau*, and five brothers, Frank, Joseph, Albert, George, and Matthew Sullivan of Waterloo, Iowa, went down with the ship. After this event, the U.S. military changed its policy regarding the assignment of blood relatives to the same military unit.

11. **Answer: D. None of the above.** World War II was the most expensive war the United States has fought to date. The Revolutionary War cost $149 million, the Spanish-American War cost $2.5 billion, and the Vietnam War cost $121.5 billion.

QUESTIONS

★ ★ ★ ★ ★ ★ ★

12. In a special ceremony on November 19, 1943, a member of the Third Infantry was awarded the Purple Heart, the Silver Star, and the Distinguished Service Medal for "bravery in action against the enemy." What was unusual about the recipient?

A. He was a Japanese spy.
B. He was a dog.
C. He had died 100 years before, and the medal was awarded posthumously.
D. He had never been in the military.

13. Associated Press photographer Joe Rosenthal won the Pulitzer prize for his February 23, 1945, image of six men, one of the most famous photographs in American history. What were these men doing?

A. Firing a tank
B. Raising a flag
C. Storming a beach
D. Riveting an airplane

14. World War II put many of America's young men in Europe and the Pacific, leaving America's women to keep the country's business and industry running. The fine job they did earned them a collective nickname. What was it?

A. Rosie the Riveter
B. Betty the Builder
C. Wilma the Welder
D. Jennie the Janitor

Answers

★ ★ ★ ★ ★ ★ ★

12. Answer: B. He was a dog. Chips was part of the K-9 Corps. His unit landed on Blue Beach east of Licata on Sicily's southern coast as the Allies were besieged by machine-gun fire. Of his own volition, Chips raced toward the hail of bullets and straight into the nest of Italian soldiers. He went for the throats of the enemy, and after a few moments they surrendered. The dog suffered powder burns and a bullet wound.

13. Answer: B. Raising a flag. The famous photo shows six soldiers straining to raise an American flag on Mount Suribachi over the island of Iwo Jima. This was the second American flag to be flown on Iwo Jima. Hours earlier, a smaller flag was placed on the mountaintop, an event captured by Marine Corps photographer Lou Lowery. When the small flag was replaced with a larger and more dramatic one, the AP photographer was there. His stirring picture went out over the wires and became one of the most often reproduced images in history.

14. Answer: A. Rosie the Riveter. Industries retooled their production for wartime products. Automakers like Ford and General Motors began making tanks, Westinghouse began to make electronics for military purposes, and Firestone retooled its rubber products for the war effort. America's women stepped in where their husbands, brothers, and boyfriends had been—working shifts around the clock to support the country's efforts against the Axis alliance.

QUESTIONS

★ ★ ★ ★ ★ ★ ★

15. Whose letter to Franklin Roosevelt in 1939 led to the development of the Manhattan Project?

A. Princeton professor Albert Einstein
B. Secretary of State Cordell Hull
C. Secretary of War Harry Woodring
D. British Prime Minister Winston Churchill

16. Just weeks after the unconditional surrender of Germany in 1945, a meeting was held in Potsdam, Germany, to set the rules for that country's recovery and restoration. What three major world powers were represented at the Potsdam Conference?

A. The United States, the Soviet Union, and Great Britain
B. Germany, Japan, and Italy
C. Great Britain, France, and Germany
D. The United States, Great Britain, and France

17. In 1942, Calvin Graham, who served on the U.S.S. *South Dakota* during the Battle of Guadalcanal, won the medal of honor and the bronze star. The government later took these honors back. Why?

A. He was only 12 years old.
B. He was a dog.
C. He was actually a woman.
D. He didn't exist.

Answers

15. Answer: A. Princeton professor Albert Einstein. After scientists had achieved nuclear fission, they drafted a letter that outlined the tremendous power released by the atomic process, as well as the enormous and deadly consequences. Einstein put his name to the letter, and it was sent to FDR. Based on the facts it presented, Roosevelt approved the Manhattan Project, which brought together the efforts of more than 600,000 people to develop the atomic bomb. Einstein later had great regrets about signing the letter.

16. Answer: A. The United States, the Soviet Union, and Great Britain. President Harry S. Truman of the United States, Soviet Premier Josef Stalin, and Britain's Prime Minister Winston Churchill met in the town of Potsdam, just north of Berlin. The British held an election during the conference, so partway through, Churchill was replaced with the newly elected British prime minister, Clement Attlee.

17. Answer: A. He was only 12 years old. Calvin Graham had lied about his age to fight in World War II, and when the truth came to light, he was dishonorably discharged. Later, his medals and honorable discharge were restored.

Questions

★ ★ ★ ★ ★ ★ ★

18. On V-J Day, September 2, 1945, the war was finally over. The entire country was elated, and New York's Times Square experienced wild celebration in the streets. Impulsively, a sailor grabbed a nurse and kissed her in the excitement. That moment was captured for all time on film and became one of the most famous wartime photos ever. Who was the photographer?

A. Ansel Adams
B. Alfred Eisenstaedt
C. Margaret Bourke-White
D. Richard Avedon

19. Tens of thousands of American soldiers deserted their duty during World War II. Of those, 2,864 were brought before a court martial. How many of these soldiers were executed?

A. 2,000
B. 862
C. 12
D. 1

20. Many people know the *Enola Gay* dropped the atomic bomb over Hiroshima. What was the name of the bomber that dropped the bomb over Nagasaki?

A. *Fat Man*
B. *Little Boy*
C. *Bock's Car*
D. *Enola Gay*

Answers

★ ★ ★ ★ ★ ★

18. **Answer: B. Alfred Eisenstaedt.** Snapping photos of the festivities for *Life* magazine, Eisenstaedt spotted a sailor running about, kissing young and old women alike. As the sailor grabbed the nurse and kissed her, Eisenstaedt clicked the shutter. Many people have since claimed to be the subjects in the photo. Eisenstaedt identified the nurse as Edith Shain, who said that Carl Muscarello is the sailor in question.

19. **Answer: D. 1.** Eddie Slovik of Detroit had a criminal record for a series of petty thefts. He had been drafted into the army but couldn't stomach the fighting, so he ran away from frontline duty. He later turned himself in expecting to be jailed, but when military reviews turned up his criminal record, he lost his chance at clemency. He became the only American soldier in World War II executed for desertion.

20. **Answer: C. *Bock's Car*.** Three days after Hiroshima, on August 9, 1945, the United States dropped the second atomic bomb over Japan. Pilot Major Charles Sweeney had flown his plane, the *Great Artiste,* on the previous mission when the *Enola Gay* dropped the bomb dubbed *Little Boy*. The *Great Artiste* dropped three canisters containing sensors to send data on the blast. When Sweeney learned the second mission would be his, he swapped planes with Captain Fred Bock to avoid the time-consuming hassle of removing the scientific measuring equipment from the *Great Artiste*. So Sweeney dropped the weapon called *Fat Man* from the belly of a plane called *Bock's Car*.

Arts and Literature

★ ★ ★ ★ ★ ★ ★ ★ ★ ★ ★ ★ ★ ★ ★

Things of beauty—words, melodies, images—have been gifts given through the years by American writers, artists, composers, and filmmakers. These creative folks have found their way into American history, and into the questions and answers of this chapter.

1. In 1820, after 15 months at sea, a Nantucket sailing ship called the *Essex* met an untimely end in the South Pacific. This tragic sinking became the inspiration for a classic American novel. What was the name of that novel?

A. *The Sea Wolf*
B. *Moby Dick*
C. *The Old Man and the Sea*
D. *Tales of the South Pacific*

2. The traditional American folk dance known as "square dancing" became the center of social gatherings in the mid-1800s. But it wasn't created full blown, of course. From what other dance style did square dancing evolve?

A. Minuet
B. Ballet
C. Cotillion
D. Native American dance

3. True or False: American film pioneer Edwin S. Porter shot his groundbreaking 1903 western, *The Great Train Robbery*, in Hollywood, California.

Answers

★ ★ ★ ★ ★ ★

1. **Answer: B. *Moby Dick*.** The whaling ship *Essex* met its fate when an enraged sperm whale rammed and sunk the 238-ton ship. Herman Melville's novel ended there, but that was just the beginning of the story for the 20 men who survived the whale's wrath in 1820. They spent months aboard three small boats and crossed more than 4,500 miles of ocean before they reached the South American coastline. Melville was a deckhand on the *Acushnet* when he met the son of one of the *Essex*'s crew.

2. **Answer: C. Cotillion.** Based on the French word for *petticoat*, the cotillion, a dance popular in France and Canada, influenced the American square dance. In a square dance, four couples arrange themselves in a square on the dance floor while a "caller," accompanied by a small string band, loudly and rhythmically shouts out various dancing directions.

3. **Answer: False.** Director Edwin S. Porter shot his masterpiece entirely in West Orange, New Jersey, at Thomas Edison's studio (called "The Black Maria") and on location. Most of the earliest American films were produced in studios in New Jersey, New York, or Chicago before the industry moved to the West Coast. In fact, Hollywood didn't even see its first actual movie studio until 1911.

QUESTIONS

★ ★ ★ ★ ★ ★ ★ ★

4. This American artist gained fame with stirring images of the Old West, work that has become known as the best of the Western theme. Who was this artist?

A. Georgia O'Keeffe
B. Winslow Homer
C. Grant Wood
D. Frederic Remington

5. Although they came from Liverpool, England, the Beatles had a huge impact on American culture in the 1960s. What American TV host first presented the Fab Four on national television?

A. Jack Paar
B. Johnny Carson
C. Ed Sullivan
D. Joe Franklin

6. Walt Whitman was a trained journalist and poet whose prose-like style helped free poetry from the constraints of rhyme and meter. Which of the following works was Whitman's primary contribution to American literature?

A. "Hiawatha"
B. "Ode to a Grecian Urn"
C. *Leaves of Grass*
D. *The Waste Land*

7. He may have been America's first hitmaker. This prolific songwriter wrote "Oh! Susanna" and "Old Folks at Home," among many others. Who was he?

A. Irving Berlin
B. Stephen Foster
C. Stephen Sondheim
D. Al Jolson

Answers

★ ★ ★ ★ ★ ★ ★

4. **Answer: D. Frederic Remington.** His work was based on his travels during the 1880s. Remington's Western sketches appeared in *Harper's Magazine*. He understood that the Wild West would soon be tamed, so he captured his images on canvas, such as "Cavalry Charge on the Western Plains," and in bronze, like "Bronco Buster."

5. **Answer: A. Jack Paar.** Many people remember first seeing the Beatles on February 9, 1964, as guests on CBS's *The Ed Sullivan Show*. The group had, however, already had its first American exposure on NBC's *The Jack Paar Program* some five weeks earlier, on January 3. While the Sullivan performance was live, the Paar show presented a film clip of a British concert from the previous November. Paar readily admits that he didn't know what he had; he showed the clip as a joke.

6. **Answer: C. *Leaves of Grass*.** First published in 1855, *Leaves of Grass* was Walt Whitman's lifelong obsession. He regularly added and changed the poems that appeared in the compilation and issued five different editions of the work before his death.

7. **Answer: B. Stephen Foster.** Before sound recording, people bought sheet music like they buy CDs today. Foster's music was hugely popular. When selling 5,000 copies made a song a hit, Foster sold 100,000. His other songs included "My Old Kentucky Home," "Camptown Races," and "Beautiful Dreamer." Foster wasn't as successful in his finances. He saw some, but not much, profit from his work and died at 37 with 38 cents in his pocket.

Questions

★ ★ ★ ★ ★ ★ ★

8. Name the American artist who helped to forge the style of art known as "pop art" by creating bold paintings that resembled large comic strips.

A. Andy Warhol
B. Roy Lichtenstein
C. Alexander Calder
D. Claes Oldenburg

9. Scott Joplin was a self-taught pianist and composer who started out playing in dance halls and bordellos, but eventually he made his name by playing at the 1893 World's Columbian Exposition in Chicago. What was the style in which Joplin composed most of his music?

A. Dixieland
B. Swing
C. Bebop
D. Ragtime

10. A few enterprising journalists early in the 20th century began to expose political corruption and abuses in business. By what name did these journalists become known?

A. Mudslingers
B. Gerrymanderers
C. Muckrakers
D. Newshounds

11. True or False: John Steinbeck's epic novel, *The Grapes of Wrath*, originally started its life as a newspaper article.

Answers

★ ★ ★ ★ ★ ★

8. Answer: B. Roy Lichtenstein. Many of his oversized paintings took on a commercial style and sometimes looked more like a newspaper ad than art. One of his most famous examples of pop art, "Whaam!," depicts a jet fighter destroying an enemy with an air-to-air rocket, all in strict comic-strip style, at a size of 5½ feet by 13 feet.

9. Answer: D. Ragtime. Scott Joplin's bouncy and melodic music style was exemplified by "Maple Leaf Rag" and "The Entertainer." Written in 1902, "The Entertainer" was featured on the soundtrack of the movie *The Sting* and was released as a single. In 1974, 57 years after Joplin's death, it reached number three on the charts.

10. Answer: C. Muckrakers. Teddy Roosevelt first used the term as an insult, likening reform-minded writers to a character in John Bunyan's *Pilgrim's Progress* "who could look no way but downward with the muck-rake in his hands; who would neither look up nor regard the crown he was offered." The movement's most successful proponents, such as Ida Tarbell, Lincoln Steffens, and Upton Sinclair, helped reign in government and business excess.

11. Answer: True. The fictional account of the Joad family, forced from their Oklahoma farm by the Dust Bowl in the 1930s, was drawn from John Steinbeck's research for a 1936 series in *The San Francisco News* called "Harvest Gypsies." When *The Grapes of Wrath* was published three years later, the book provoked both great popular acclaim and strong condemnation for its depiction of Oklahoma migrants and California growers.

Questions

★ ★ ★ ★ ★ ★ ★

12. Writer/director Orson Welles shook up Hollywood and the country (not to mention the Hearst family) when he released the cinematic masterpiece *Citizen Kane* in 1941. What was the intended original title of the film?

A. *American*
B. *The Publisher*
C. *Hearst Castle*
D. *Only in the United States*

13. George M. Cohan, originally a vaudeville performer, became one of the most successful writers and performers on Broadway during the first half of the 20th century. Which of these Cohan musicals introduced his hit songs "I'm a Yankee Doodle Dandy" and "Give My Regards to Broadway"?

A. *Little Johnny Jones*
B. *Forty-Five Minutes From Broadway*
C. *Song and Dance Man*
D. *The Merry Malones*

14. Film director Martin Scorsese is best known for his gritty, New York-based themes, seen in movies such as *Taxi Driver*, *Raging Bull*, and *Goodfellas*. How many Academy Awards has Scorsese won for Best Director?

A. One
B. Two
C. Three
D. Zero

Answers

★ ★ ★ ★ ★ ★

12. **Answer: A. *American*.** Orson Welles crafted the screenplay with Herman J. Mankiewicz, figuring that a somewhat fictionalized version of American newspaper magnate William Randolph Hearst was a suitable subject for the film. Hearst was none too pleased with having details of his life splattered across the silver screen, so he did everything he could to keep the film from being released. When that didn't work, he ordered that none of the Hearst newspapers carry any ads for the film. Although a financial failure upon its release, *Citizen Kane* has come to be considered one of the best American films ever made.

13. **Answer: A. *Little Johnny Jones*.** George M. Cohan's first big show, *Little Johnny Jones*, debuted in 1903. In it, Cohan played the show title's horse jockey. Contrary to his claim of being "born on the 4th of July," Cohan was actually born on July 3. At least he was close.

14. **Answer: D. Zero.** Hard to believe, but Martin Scorsese, the man who many have called "America's greatest living film director," has never won an Oscar for directing. Nominated three times for Best Director, Scorsese is adept at showing the seedier sides of people's lives in films like *Mean Streets*, *King of Comedy*, and *Casino*. Yet, he can also present gentle and sensitive works of film, such as *Age of Innocence* and *Kundun*.

QUESTIONS

★ ★ ★ ★ ★ ★ ★

15. It's a very famous painting by a famous artist, but very few people know its actual title. Who painted *Arrangement in Gray and Black No. 1*?

A. Grandma Moses
B. Winslow Homer
C. James Whistler
D. Andy Warhol

16. Ernest Hemingway was one of the most well-known and successful novelists of the 20th century, receiving international recognition in winning the Nobel Prize for Literature in 1954. Which of these American novels was NOT written by Hemingway?

A. *A Farewell to Arms*
B. *To Have and Have Not*
C. *For Whom the Bell Tolls*
D. *The Sound and the Fury*

17. In 1935, a singing group named the Hoboken Four appeared on radio's *Major Bowes' Amateur Hour* and won the performance contest. While the Hoboken Four never reached stardom, one of its members did. Who was this famous singer?

A. Mel Torme
B. Frank Sinatra
C. Ella Fitzgerald
D. Tony Bennett

ANSWERS

★ ★ ★ ★ ★ ★ ★

15. Answer: C. James Whistler. This painting is more commonly known by its unofficial title: *Whistler's Mother*. Whistler was born in Massachusetts and spent three years at the Military Academy at West Point, but he did poorly in his studies and left West Point to study art. The artist spent most of his career in Europe, painting and doing etchings in Paris and London. He also became known for his skills as an interior decorator before his death in 1903.

16. Answer: D. *The Sound and the Fury.* While the other three were written by Ernest "Papa" Hemingway, *The Sound and the Fury* was written in 1929 by another renowned 20th-century novelist, William Faulkner (who won his own Nobel Prize for Literature in 1949). Faulkner wrote mostly about the world he knew: the American South and its people. He would eventually write Hollywood screenplays in the 1940s, such as *To Have and Have Not* and *The Big Sleep*.

17. Answer: B. Frank Sinatra. Sinatra was a native of Hoboken, New Jersey. The vocal group auditioned for the show as Frank Sinatra and the 3 Flashes. Sinatra soon went solo, singing with the big bands of Harry James and Tommy Dorsey. In the '40s he became a pop icon, causing teenage girls to swoon and teenage boys to become insanely jealous. Sinatra also appeared in films, winning an Academy Award in 1953 for *From Here to Eternity*. "Ol' Blue Eyes" became larger than life, calling his own shots in public and private life, until he died in 1998.

QUESTIONS

★ ★ ★ ★ ★ ★ ★

18. Robert Frost was America's most beloved poet in the 20th century, a position that became assured when he read at the presidential inauguration of John F. Kennedy, the first poet ever to read on such an occasion. How old was Frost when his first collection of poetry, *A Boy's Will*, was published?

A. 17
B. 23
C. 30
D. 39

19. Painting in America has seen a number of different styles come and go throughout its history. One prominent style of painting has been Abstract Expressionism. One particular form of Abstract Expressionism was "drip art." What American painter of the 1950s was a master of the "dripping" style of painting?

A. Man Ray
B. Jackson Pollock
C. Robert Rauschenberg
D. Frank Stella

20. American symphonic composer Charles Ives was a realist who understood that many classical composers couldn't make a living composing. In what occupation did Ives earn his money?

A. As a teacher
B. As a bus driver
C. As an insurance executive
D. As a commercial jingle writer

Answers

★ ★ ★ ★ ★ ★

18. **Answer: D. 39.** Although Robert Frost had been writing poetry since he was in high school, he had been unable to get much of his work published in this country. In 1912 he moved with his wife and family to England, where his luck quickly changed. *A Boy's Will* was published in England the next year, with a follow-up published the year after that, and in 1915 Frost returned to America a renowned poet. He continued writing for the rest of his life.

19. **Answer: B. Jackson Pollock.** According to rival artist Willem de Kooning, "Jackson broke the ice" for Abstract Expressionism. Pollock would lay large canvases on the floor of his Long Island studio and pour or splash paint out of the can in an animated fashion. Some critics viewed his work as impulsive and untrained, but many regarded it as brilliant, dynamic art. The master of "drip art" died in a car accident in 1956.

20. **Answer: C. As an insurance executive.** Charles Ives composed many pieces, including four symphonies, using clashing dissonance and competing rhythms. But in 1906 he also founded the insurance company of Ives and Myrick. One of his innovations in the insurance business was the development of estate planning.